MOUNTAIN RESCUE

HISTORY AND DEVELOPMENT IN THE PEAK DISTRICT 1920s–PRESENT DAY

MOUNTAIN RESCUE

HISTORY AND DEVELOPMENT IN THE PEAK DISTRICT 1920s–PRESENT DAY

IAN HURST &
ROGER BENNETT

Proceeds from the sale of this book will go to support mountain rescue in the Peak District.

First published in 2007 by Tempus Publishing

Reprinted in 2009 by
The History Press
The Mill, Brimscombe Port,
Stroud, Gloucestershire, GL5 2QG
www.thehistorypress.co.uk

British Library Cataloguing in Publication Data.
A catalogue record for this book is available from the British Library.

ISBN 978 0 7524 4091 0

Printed in Great Britain

CONTENTS

CALL OUT THE MOUNTAIN RESCUE

Call out the Mountain Rescue!
I came up for a lark,
But the night is getting chilly,
And the fells are getting dark,
My shoe's lost its stiletto heel,
My frock is feeling thin,
Call out the Mountain Rescue,
And let's get taken in.

Call out the Mountain Rescue!
To search the hills and vales,
Swathed in ropes and cables,
Like a team of Chippendales,
Release the search–and–rescue dogs!
They'll find me by my smell,
I ate a Kendal Mint Cake,
And I'm wearing my Chanel.

Call out the Mountain Rescue!
I am stranded on a crag,
My hairstyle's badly damaged,
And I've snapped my shoulder-bag,
I'm utterly exhausted,
Cannot move another inch,
So hail the helicopter!
I am ready for the winch.

Call out the Mountain Rescue!
Wrap me warm and well,
Lay me on a stretcher-bed,
And bear me down the fell,
Heal me with your tenderness,
Drench me with your sorrow,
Drop me off at home,
I'll call you out again tomorrow.

FOREWORD

It is with great pleasure that I write a few words about this book and mountain rescue in the Peak District.

This book chronicles the history and development of the mountain rescue service here in the Peak District, from one of the first recorded incidents in 1911 up to the present day. Some of the earliest rescuers were the local police constables together with the local watermen, quarry men, farmers and gamekeepers. The latter may well have been employed by my great grandfather who owned large parts of Kinder Scout at the time.

They were not trained or indeed equipped to deliver first aid or abseil down cliffs, but they provided aid to their fellow man as the need arose as humanitarians.

This book takes the reader from those early days to the present-day service and is a fascinating record of little-known facts and stories that can so easily be lost in time.

I admire the young men and women volunteers of our rescue teams who are fully committed to helping those in difficulty in the Peak District hills and dales. They turn out at a moment's notice, often in cold, wet or snowy conditions on operations when the rest of us would prefer to curl up in a warm bed. They have terrific skills and knowledge and are dedicated to their task. Additionally, they spend many hours training and even more raising much-needed funds for their own specialist equipment in order to provide the best care and pre-hospital support. Some fundraising is undertaken here at Chatsworth.

I also recognise that they are called upon increasingly more frequently year on year; this I am assured is not due to us becoming less responsible for our own actions, but probably due to the increasing numbers of people taking part in more active recreational pursuits.

The Peak District is a beautiful place to visit, walk or climb and is more accessible than ever before. This should be cherished and your visit fondly remembered but be assured that this wonderful service is available should you need to call for it.

Devonshire

His Grace, The Duke of Devonshire, CBE
Chatsworth

His Grace, The Duke of Devonshire, CBE.
(© Bill Burlington)

PREFACE

It is a great honour to be the first president of the Peak District Mountain Rescue Organisation (PDMRO) and to be associated with a team of wonderful people who do an outstanding job in ensuring the safety of the public in the Peak District and beyond. The public has good reason to be grateful for the support and skill of PDMRO members, and members of the Search and Rescue Dogs Association, SARDA, freely given for over forty years. Although the police have a great deal of experience and professional skill in search and recovery, the experience and knowledge of the many MR and SARDA members and their ability to search vast areas of difficult terrain quickly and thoroughly is an invaluable resource to us. Their search skills have to be seen to be believed! That is why I and many of my Chief Constable colleagues do everything we can to support and sustain Mountain Rescue activity in this country, and I have previously recognised the organisation by means of a formal Chief Constable's Commendation, a rare award which is reserved for service of the highest quality.

Many thousands of people visit and enjoy our beautiful Peak District each year, quite rightly free to roam as they will. I suspect few of them give more than a passing thought to the professional and voluntary back-up systems that exist, ready to come to their assistance if they get into difficulties. Mountain Rescue, like policing, is embedded in the national psyche, almost regarded as a right, and people just assume it will be there for them. They feel very secure when out walking, that someone is there to help them should they need it; sometimes, I think, too secure, because many fail to take adequate precautions to ensure their own safety, not necessarily through being irresponsible, but simply through failing to understand the vagaries of remote terrain, and the rapidity with which weather conditions can change in the High Peak. But it is not only in rugged terrain that the PDMRO operates. They readily respond to calls from police forces around the region to help search for missing people in open country and the urban fringe, and they help save many lives, particularly of elderly and vulnerable people missing in poor weather conditions.

Much like the police service that I have been part of for nearly thirty-two years now, people usually only see the 'front end' of the PDMRO's service, and mostly only when it involves them. Very few people actually know a great deal about what it is really like. What they do not see is the hours of training, the imposition on family commitments, the domestic disruption, the missed meals, the exposure to physical danger and risk, the sheer stress of being responsible for the safety of others, and the cost in financial terms, both individually and collectively, that members willingly give to be part of this wonderful enterprise. Perhaps, on the upside, they also do not realise the fantastic buzz that members get out of using their skills helping people in distress, the sense of purpose and belonging, of contributing to society, the camaraderie of the teams, and the sheer joy of being out in our natural surroundings, even when the weather is doing its worst.

In Derbyshire alone, records show that in the last twelve months, MR teams have rescued people aged from eight to eighty-five years, attended accidents involving canoes, sledges, bicycles and paragliding, and helped find a number of vulnerable missing people.

An example of their commitment and dedication was on Christmas Day 2006 when a call came in about a seventy-year-old man lost near Grindleford, shortly after 5 p.m., when most of us were at home with our families full of turkey, mince pies and wine.

David Coleman, QPM, BA (Hons)
Chief Constable Derbyshire Constabulary and president of the Peak District Mountain Rescue Organisation.

Sixty members turned out that day and after four hours of searching, found him suffering from exposure. What an achievement! There is no doubt in my mind what would have happened to that man without the help of the PDMRO.

But the PDMRO cannot continue to deliver such excellent service without the means to support the provision and maintenance of bases, transport, equipment, running costs, and insurance premiums. Somehow we need to find better ways of engaging the public – particularly the walking and climbing public – and potential sponsors, to help people understand just what a marvellous service they have and how little funding it gets from official sources. PDMRO members are proud of their voluntary status, and most would not want to be part of a Government-funded organisation. Members come to Mountain Rescue mostly from a passionate personal interest in outdoor pursuits, and so naturally they value their freedom and independence. There is a great deal to be said about the volunteer tradition, and we must fight to preserve this wonderful service. I want to help in that endeavour, and would very much welcome a discussion with anyone who feels they can offer financial or other support to the PDMRO.

David Coleman, QPM, BA (Hons)
Chief Constable, Derbyshire Constabulary
President of the Peak District Mountain Rescue Organisation

THE AUTHORS

Roger Bennett was born in Stockport and had his first taste of hill walking aged thirteen on visits to Kinder Scout with school friends via the bus to Hayfield. At the age of fifteen he walked the Pennine Way with three schoolmates.

Serving as a police officer with the Cheshire Constabulary from 1969 to 1979, Roger was also a voluntary National Park warden 1969–73. His first involvement with mountain rescue came through this warden service and Edale Mountain Rescue Team in the early 1970s.

In 1977 he joined Buxton Mountain Rescue Team whilst serving as rural beat police officer in Macclesfield Forest, becoming team leader 1989–94 and representing the Peak District at Mountain Rescue (England and Wales) for fifteen years.

In 2003 he was awarded the Queen's Jubilee Medal and is currently a Trustee and Honorary Treasurer of Buxton team.

Ian Hurst joined the Peak District National Park Warden Service as a voluntary warden in 1963 and was a member of the team that located and recovered the body of John Butterfield from Alport in March 1964.

Ian was a member of Edale MRT from 1963 to 1971 and a full-time Peak District National Park warden/ranger from 1970 up until 2007. He also served as Honorary Secretary, Honorary Treasurer and Honorary Insurance Officer for the Peak District Mountain Rescue Organisation, being appointed a Peak District Mountain Rescue Organisation controller in 1971, a role he continues today.

In 1984 he received two commendations from the RSPCA for sheep rescues from cliffs in Water Cum Jolly Dale. He has also received the Derbyshire Constabulary Chief Constables Commendation for Mountain Rescue and was awarded the Queen's Jubilee Medal in 2003.

Ian is currently a Trustee of Mountain Rescue (England and Wales) and has held the post of chairman of Buxton MRT since 1991.

ACKNOWLEDGEMENTS

Ian and Roger are not professional authors but have simply attempted to record for posterity the origins of mountain rescue in the Peak District before early records and memories are lost forever. Every effort has been made to check the accuracy of the information contained in the book but we apologise in advance for any discrepancies. Many, many people have played a part in building the current organisation and it would be impossible to mention every name or describe every event. The book is dedicated to all those who have given their time, effort and money to support mountain rescue and is a memorial to those unfortunate few who lost their lives on the hills of the Peak District.

This book could not have been written without the help and support of a great number of people and we wish to thank them for their assistance. We have also been given access to a wide variety of records and publications during our research into the story of the Peak District Mountain Rescue Organisation. We acknowledge the contributors' generous agreement to permit publication of their material in this book without charge in the knowledge that any profits from its sale will be donated to the support of mountain rescue.

Special thanks are proffered to: Gaynor Andrew; Keith Bell; Malc Bowyer; Derek Bunting; Buxton Mountain Rescue Team; *The Buxton Advertiser*; Neil Carruthers, Charles Chesters; John Coombs; Pat Cunningham; Ray Davies; Derby Mountain Rescue Team; Edale Mountain Rescue Team; John Fielding; Mike France; Glossop Mountain Rescue Team; Liz Hamilton; Mike Hammond; Steve Harrington; Karen Harrison; Howard Hodgkinson; Tony Hood; Peter Hyde; David Kirkpatrick; Robin Knott; Rod Leach; John Mayer; Gordon Miller; Eric Needham; Oldham Mountain Rescue Team; Peak District National Park Authority; Royton Air Training Corps; Gerry Rawson; *The Sheffield Telegraph*; Roly Smith; Di Tranter; Deana Wheatley; Bob Whitall; Mike Williams; Woodhead Mountain Rescue Team.

This is not a technical handbook but a story which everyone who ventures into the great outdoors should read.

INTRODUCTION

The Peak District Mountain Rescue Organisation (PDMRO) has provided a service to the local community and to visitors to the Peak District National Park since 1964. To some the use of the term 'mountain' may seem a little extravagant when describing the topography of the region as no part lies over 636m (2,088ft) above sea level. But those who know its wild side, its plateaux of deep peat bogs swept by biting east winds or enveloped in swirling cloud and rain, know that the moors can be every bit as threatening, tiring and lonely as any of the classic mountains in the UK. So it is then that those who make up the ranks of the seven rescue teams in the Peak District have no embarrassment about using the title 'Mountain Rescue'.

The aim of this book is to record the story of the development of mountain rescue in the Peak District. The establishment of police, fire and ambulance services is governed by acts of parliament but there is no such legislation stipulating the formation of mountain rescue teams. Those who pioneered the rescue service would have no concept of what would build from their foundations and would probably even have shunned such a fanciful phrase as mountain rescue. It was a natural development and reflected the changes in public use of the land, the necessities of war, technical improvements to clothing and equipment and the encouragement of the police and other professional services. It developed, not in isolation, but alongside other regions of the country and was led by the inspirations of many people dedicated to helping those in distress in the hills.

The aims of the organisation have never changed and search and rescue in the hills and dales is still its primary role, but in modern times the teams now play a wider role in assisting the police and ambulance services.

If today you were to start with a blank piece of paper and attempt to design a rescue organisation for the Peak District, you may not arrive at what is the current system, with the seven teams in the areas that they now cover. However, local rescue teams grew up independently and then banded together under a regional umbrella. There was never any master plan, no government or legislative framework and no central funding agency to control the purse strings. The system developed year on year with teams dissolving, amalgamating and emerging as the forces of need, finance and commonsense prevailed. What is left is not perfect but the changes are ongoing and the organisation will continue to adapt to the requirements and expectations of the day.

Like its six sister organisations in England and Wales, the PDMRO was born simply from a local need for an organised response to calls for assistance when someone got into difficulties in the remoter parts of the national park. Note the word organised, for there were rescue teams in the area long before the formation of the PDMRO and, when the cry for assistance went up there was certainly no shortage of willing volunteers offering help. However, whilst enthusiasm was not lacking, some of the skills, experience and certainly equipment were in short supply. But these were the formative days when the skills taken for granted today were still being learnt and equipment consisted of what could be begged or borrowed rather than today's specially designed and sophisticated paraphernalia.

Some of the participants in those early rescues are still active in today's modern rescue service and the authors are grateful for their assistance in writing this book. However, when they reflect

When the summer crowds have gone home the winter brings peace and solitude.

on their early experiences of rescue they must find it difficult to compare the lightweight equipment, speed of communications and the casualty care skills of today's teams with those of just forty years ago.

The teams remain as independent charities that choose to come together regionally as the PDMRO and likewise each of the seven regions in England and Wales affiliates to the national umbrella body of Mountain Rescue (England and Wales). Together, the fifty-one teams have a membership of some 3,000 volunteers and can boast of being one of the largest voluntary organisations in the UK without a single paid or employed member. The service they offer can be as professional as any of the full-time emergency services and their voluntary status demonstrates their dedication to the cause.

Each team has to raise its own funds by whatever means it can. An annual grant from the National Health Service to the national council provides an average of £300-worth of medical supplies for each team. But when you consider that just the running costs of a team can be up to £35,000 per annum, then £300 does not go very far. Capital expenditure on buildings and vehicles adds an even greater burden.

There is no central pot of money, no government grant and no national trust fund to fall back on. Every pound spent by a team is raised by that team without the help of employed fundraisers or administrators. Whilst some teams provide limited outer shell clothing for their members the majority of other clothing and equipment has to be bought by the members themselves. Add to that the expense of travelling to incidents, training events and meetings, and the cost to the individual becomes very significant.

Geographically, Derbyshire dominates the Peak District National Park, as over half of the county is within the park, but there are also significant slices of Cheshire, Staffordshire, Greater

Manchester and South and West Yorkshire within the boundary. Each county has its own police service and fire and rescue service and used to have its own ambulance service but recent regional amalgamations have reduced these to four across the park.

One of the main accomplishments of the PDMRO has been to encourage all these separate organisations to recognise the logic of having one common rescue service for the remote areas of the region and to convince them that a group of unpaid volunteers can actually do the job they claim to be able to do. It has taken many years and a great deal of dedication by all those involved to build the confidence and trust that now exists between the volunteers and the professionals.

Just forty years ago private telephones were still quite a novelty and a team leader may have had to call out his team by driving to each member's house, knocking to get him or her out of bed, waiting for him or her to dress and then drive onto the next member's house. Radios were non-existent or at least not available to civilian volunteer teams, equipment was heavy with liberal use of canvas and steel and clothing was also heavy, not very waterproof and often ex-army.

In the event of an injury to someone high on the moors, it may have taken three or more hours for a companion to come off the hill and find a telephone box or farm from which to contact the police. Now a mobile phone message alerts the police or ambulance control within seconds. The rescue team's call-out officer simply sends one electronic message and the whole team is instantly alerted by radio-pager or text and can make its way to the chosen rendezvous point.

Litigation, legislation and funding are today's challenges to all voluntary bodies, and particularly so to rescue teams working, at times, in risky situations and poor weather conditions. In the 1960s a team may have spent less than £100 a year on running costs but this was enough because the walking world knew that those coming to their aid were ramblers themselves and casualties did not expect fancy treatment. Now the public expects a fast and effective service from people dressed, equipped and trained to do the job.

Most people think that the rescue service is professional and part of some other emergency service. Mountain rescue has perhaps been its own worst enemy in this sense as it continues to promote itself in a more professional manner and tries to emulate its full-time counterparts. The cost is a spiralling financial burden and an increased toll on the team member's personal time as he or she struggles to fit in the extra training to meet the demands of certification. With the average annual cost of maintaining a team now around £25,000, how long the teams can remain independent and totally voluntary is anybody's guess. However, it looks likely that the service will always remain available and whilst volunteers run it, the service will remain free at the point of need.

There have been many improvements in the rescue service but the terrain and weather have hardly altered, despite global warming. Minus 5 degrees is still as cold as it ever was and the bogs are still just as deep and wet. The moors and crags of the Peak District have claimed many lives and they still wait to catch the unwary or unprepared visitor.

The modern PDMRO is a tribute to those who worked and strived so hard in the early days to keep improving the help that could be offered to those in distress in our local hills. It was their patience, their energy and their tenacity that laid the foundations for a rescue service that has since been officially recognised many times for its professionalism and dedication.

ONE

SOCIAL CLIMBING: THE 1850S ONWARD

Our story has to start with the explosion in social rambling and climbing and an understanding of the forces that encouraged people to take to the hills for recreation. Mountain Rescue was born from a need, and without people going to the hills for the simple joys of the fresh air and freedom there would be no need.

Since the coming of the railways in the late nineteenth century the Peak District has been a Mecca for all who have sought the peace and tranquillity or the challenge and adventure of the great outdoors. Wealthy individuals and gentlemen's walking clubs were some of the first to seek a breath of country air away from the fast-growing and increasingly populated industrial towns surrounding the area. However, it was the network of railways, built to take the coal, limestone, milk and livestock into the ever-consuming and demanding centres of industrialisation, that led to the provision of cheap transport for the working classes to escape the smog and grime of the town for a day in the country.

Rambling clubs grew in popularity as the social benefits of an organised, guided walk were realised, and particularly so when there was the chance of a singsong and a bottle of beer on the way home. Some clubs sprang from religious beginnings whilst others had more political roots, and some, like the Sheffield Clarion Ramblers' Club, simply from an individual love of the freedom of the outdoors publicly inviting others to come along.

The end of the First World War brought a new flush of enthusiasm to spend time away from the cities, and by the 1920s–30s the pastime of hiking had increased to such proportions that special trains and buses were laid on at weekends to the villages at the heart of the area such as Edale, Hayfield and Woodhead. However, all who came to the Peak District encountered the same problem, that of restricted access to the upper and more remote parts of the district. The moors and remoter crags were all private and jealously guarded by their owners against the intrusion of so many feet on the sacred home of the grouse. Grouse shooting was big business, not so much for the harvest of slaughtered birds, but for the considerable sum of money that wealthy individuals would pay for a gun day.

EARLY DAYS AND EARLY RESCUES

Walking and indeed climbing are not in themselves dangerous occupations if a few basic principles are adhered to. However, the chance of an accident could never be ruled out and, with a primitive map and compass, the risk of a navigational mistake was always present. Thus, with visitor numbers increasing, accidents and other incidents began to be reported. However, one of the earliest recorded incidents did not involve a visitor but a five-year-old boy named Ehoy Sandells from Hayfield.

The event was fully described in *The Reporter* on 28 April 1911 under the headline, 'Lost on the Scout'. Ehoy was last seen playing with other children near the Hayfield Waterworks before he was chased away by workmen. He failed to return home. Constables Tipper and Bell made enquiries that evening but were unable to locate him, so a search was organised for the following morning. The constables and fourteen workmen from the reservoir met at 05.00 a.m. and started a search of William

Well-dressed walkers pose for a photograph in the lower reaches of Grindsbrook near Edale around the 1930s. Although no guns are evident it is possible they were actually part of a grouse shooting party. Note the tie and watch chain!

Two ramblers look towards the summit of Kinder Scout on a winter's day.

Before the negotiation of access agreements much of the Peak District was under private ownership and it was necessary to gain special permission before ramblers or climbers could venture onto the land. This letter, dated October 1932, is from Sir Philip Brocklehurst, then owner of The Roaches, in which he reluctantly gives permission for Miss Mary Glynne to climb on the crag for one day:

Oct 21st '32

Miss Mary Glynne –

I regret the delay in replying to your letter as I have been away and just returned. I have closed the Roaches to all climbing clubs on account of the nuisance it was becoming – so many clubs including it in their annual programme, taking permission for granted and as it is the main part of my grouse moor it became quite impossible as such, when people were always on it. If I give you permission this time as you are not a club, I cannot promise you permission again. Besides I need a clerk to reply to all the requests and it's best to allow it to be known that permits are not given.

Yours faithfully
Philip Brocklehurst

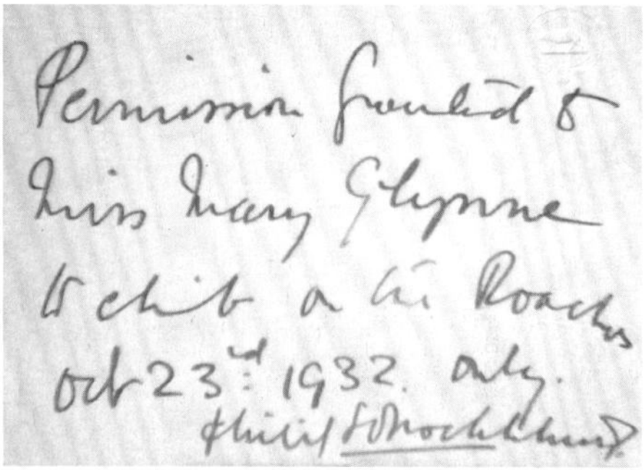

This card, signed by Brocklehurst, could be shown to the local gamekeeper if challenged:

> Permission granted to Miss Mary Glynne to climb on the Roaches Oct 23rd 1932 only.
> Philip Brocklehurst

Clough and the Upper House areas. The lad was later found safe and well below Kinder Downfall and, after being given an orange, he was returned home apparently no worse for his experience.

In November the same year the headline of *The Reporter* featured 'Three People Missing on Kinder'. When the three were eventually found the newspaper chronicled their plight:

> Having followed the Kinder River for half a mile southward we faced an apparently interminable sea of black crevasses capped with snow and looking like waves. As soon as we plunged into the crevasses our lady companion, hitherto imperturbable, suddenly lost all her nerve and she fell in to a heap and stretched herself out in the snow moaning and begging us to leave her there.

The three were benighted on the moor but finally arrived at their destination safe but exhausted.

In later years the newspapers recorded more incidents and sometimes in tragic circumstances. *The Reporter*, on 8 January 1922 led with the story of a rambler named Henry Fowler Martin being found dead on Kinder Scout having succumbed to the weather after being missing for a week. On Sunday 11 February 1922 a Mr Edwin Newton from Ashton under Lyne went walking on Kinder Scout and failed to return. For a fortnight a large body of searchers, including his friends, shepherds and gamekeepers, swept the bleak snow-covered moors in an effort to find him. Fifteen days after his disappearance his body was found with a fractured skull near Kinder Downfall and it was presumed he had fallen from the ice-covered rocks.

Concern was already being expressed that such incidents were increasing and that the response was generally poorly co-ordinated in terms of any search. The matter was highlighted in January 1925 when Mr James Evans from Levenshulme in Manchester, a member of the Manchester Rambling Club, went walking on the 4th and failed to return. The then *Manchester Guardian* newspaper put out an appeal for experienced ramblers to gather at meeting points in Glossop, Hayfield and Edale in order to mount a search of Kinder Scout, and stated, 'Search parties will be allowed cheap bookings on the train between Manchester London Road Station and Glossop

Opposite: A police 'Missing from Home' poster issued by Ashton under Lyne Borough Police. Edwin Newton was a schoolmaster and renowned walker from Ashton and was reputed to walk between thirty and fifty miles on each of his regular tramps. On Sunday 11 February 1922 he left home to visit the grave of his friend Henry Martin who had died in a fall on Kinder Scout only a month earlier and was now buried at Hayfield. When he failed to return it was presumed he had visited the church and then gone for a walk on the moors. Initially local police and gamekeepers carried out a search but nothing was found. During the intervening week local rambling clubs and scout organisations were contacted and the following weekend a large search was co-ordinated. Still the body of Mr Newton could not be found and it was not until the

ASHTON-UNDER-LYNE BOROUGH POLICE

Telephone: No. 2 Ashton

Chief Constable's Office,
Ashton-under-Lyne, February 14th, 1922.

PHOTOGRAPH and DESCRIPTION of

EDWIN NEWTON

MISSING

From his home, Blandford Street, Ashton-under-Lyne, since 12 p.m., Saturday, February 11th, 1922.

Age - - 48 Years.
Height - 5 ft. 9 or 10 ins.
Build - - Strong.
Complexion, Fresh.

When he left home, the missing man was dressed in a dark grey Knickerbocker uit, grey Stockings, strong Boots, a fawn Raincoat, and carried a Walking Stick.

He was last seen at Guidebridge Station soon after noon on Saturday, and he then idicated that it was his intention to visit the Cemetery at Hayfield.

Mr. Newton has acted as traveller for a Confectionery Firm, of which he is a iember. He is well known in the Peakland district as a walker.

He has recently had an attack of influenza, and may be suffering from loss of iemory.

Please cause enquiries to be made at all likely places in your district, and if met ith, please detain and communicate with

H. A. TOLSON,
Chief Constable, Ashton-under-Lyne,
Manchester Central Police Station, or
Hayfield Police Station.

next weekend, when a massive search was undertaken, that he was located near to Kinder Downfall just 300 yards from where his friend Henry Martin had fallen. The search had consisted of thirty members of the Ashton clubs and a large number from the Manchester clubs walking in from Hayfield, together with a large contingent from the Sheffield clubs searching from Edale. The body was found by Mr Norman Dawson, also from Ashton, lying on a rocky ledge under the Downfall. The area had been searched before but the position of the body made it difficult to locate. Word was quickly sent to Hayfield Police Station and officers returned with a stretcher and ropes. Newspaper reports record 'officers had to be dragged up the rocks to examine the body'.

Classic Kinder Scout weather! Even when the sun shines in the valley the mist can suddenly descend and the air temperature dramatically drop. This photograph shows the Ordnance Survey triangulation pillar at Kinder Low. The pillar is one of three on Kinder Scout that thousands of walkers have been grateful to see and be able to positively establish their position on the map. The pillars are no longer used by the Ordnance Survey and their future is now in doubt, although some have been adopted by local groups which have pledged to maintain them.

A classic view of Kinder Downfall in the depths of winter when the waterfall has frozen, providing a rare opportunity for ice-climbing in the Peak District.

and additionally on trains to Hayfield', although it was pointed out that such privileges were for bona fide searchers only! Mr Eustace Thomas, president of the Rucksack Club, would be in charge from the Edale side whilst the police and the Manchester Rambling Club would order operations from Hayfield. The newspaper continued its comment on the incident with a report from its special correspondent in Hayfield saying, 'There is a need for a co-ordinated rescue scheme to be supervised by the police.' However, there were not enough people taking part and the Ramblers' Federation, which had fifty member clubs to call upon, was asked to 'look at devising an emergency plan whereby the required number of walkers could present themselves for a human quest'. Mr Evans's body was found on 10 January and the coroner confirmed his death from exposure to the elements.

It may have been as a direct result of this incident that the *Ramblers' Handbook* of 1927 ran an article on search organisation by J. Lloyd. It is presumed that this is the same Mr Lloyd of Reddish, Stockport, who had been instrumental in organising the search for Mr Edwin Newton in February 1922. The report talks of the setting up of a 'rapid search committee' and a 'district mapping committee' to enable search parties to be found and directed to selected areas. These committees were to be responsible for calling out volunteers from local rambling clubs by placing an advert in the Manchester newspapers. The article also referred to the need for some of the searchers to be qualified in first aid and suggested that courses should be organised by the Ramblers' Federation.

The search committee had a busy first year managing at least three incidents. The first involved about 200 volunteers in a search of Greenfield near Oldham. For the second one preparations were made to assemble searchers at Disley to look for a Stockport man, but this was called off as he was found before the appointed meeting time. The third incident occurred during the General Strike so transport for the searchers was one of the first problems to be dealt with.

However, transport problems must have seemed insignificant when compared with the question of where to start looking. According to the Manchester Federation's report the area to be searched included the whole of Derbyshire and part of Cheshire. The 'telephone' was used to contact a number of police stations throughout Derbyshire and eventually small search parties set out from Edale, Hayfield, Castleton and Chapel en le Frith. The records show that the lady in question was located at Rowarth near New Mills but they do not indicate any detail of the circumstances. Unfortunately the authors cannot find any further records of this committee's activities; perhaps the thought of searching all Derbyshire and part of Cheshire was too daunting!

Whilst there are early reports of missing people and mass searches of the Peak District hills there are few records of any accidents. Before 1935 a walker succumbing to a broken leg or even worse was at the mercy of the capability of his friends to administer what first aid they could and then to carry him off by whatever means was available. Stories are told of farm gates being used as makeshift stretchers and jackets being stretched between signposts declaring that 'Trespassers will be prosecuted' to improvise a carry-off. Most walkers at this time would be out as part of a club or federation so presumably there would be plenty of willing hands to assist in the evacuation. Certainly there were no formal rescue teams available and if extra help was needed it usually fell to local shepherds and gamekeepers to assist.

TWO

THE REAL BEGINNING

One accident, in 1928 on Laddow Rocks, above Crowden Great Brook in the Peak District, has taken a significant place in the history of mountain rescue.

Members of the Rucksack Club were climbing on Long Climb, a 55ft gritstone route graded as Very Difficult, when Edgar Pryor, a club member, was knocked from his stance by a falling climber and suffered a broken leg. Laddow Rocks are not particularly elevated but they are about two miles from the nearest road. Mr Pryor's friends improvised a stretcher from a metal rucksack frame and a farm gate and the evacuation commenced. Wilson Hey, later to become chairman of the Mountain Rescue Committee, attended the accident and assisted in the medical care both during the evacuation and later in hospital. Hey later recalled, 'The rescue of Pryor was an agonising business in spite of the utmost care when using an improvised splint.' Also at the scene of the accident was Herbert Hartley, later to become secretary of the Mountain Rescue Committee, who helped in the carry-off of Pryor by arranging a relay of runners to collect hot-water bottles from Crowden and take them back up to Laddow Rocks. Despite the care and attention of his friends Edgar Pryor was later to lose his leg through amputation.

The accident had been witnessed by some influential members of the Rucksack Club who decided on a course of action that was to shape the future of mountain rescue in the UK. They realised that even a proper ambulance stretcher would have been of little use in the circumstances and started discussing the possibility of improving the situation.

The Rucksack Club formed a sub-committee in 1932, consisting of B.S. Harlow and A.S. Pigott and gave it the task of finding a casualty stretcher suitable for such rescues. No stretcher could be found on the market that met the specifications but in the following year they learnt that C.P. Lapage and H.L. Pollitt of the Fell and Rock Climbing Club were making the same investigations. The Rucksack Club and the Fell and Rock Climbing Club joined forces and were instrumental in creating a sub-committee to develop a special stretcher that could easily be carried and handled in rough terrain. The 'Joint Stretcher Committee' was formed in 1933 and comprised Dr C.P. Lapage (chairman), B.S. Harlow, Wilson Hey, A.S. Pigott, H.L. Pollitt, Eustace Thomas and R. Burns. The members were a good mix of medical men and engineers and they were able to take advantage of some earlier work such as a 1931 prototype design by a Dr and Mrs Wakefield.

1935: THE JOINT STRETCHER COMMITTEE AND FIRST-AID POSTS

A report was published by the Joint Stretcher Committee in 1935 and gave details of a design for a suitable stretcher that was to become known as the Thomas Stretcher, named after Eustace Thomas, whose engineering skills and manufacturing resources were freely given. The report also gave a comprehensive list of equipment and first-aid supplies that should be available in case of mountain accidents. The report and a letter was circulated to all walking/climbing clubs and other organisations with an interest in mountaineering, and asked for their assistance in providing this equipment. The proposal was for a stretcher and other equipment to be stored at suitable

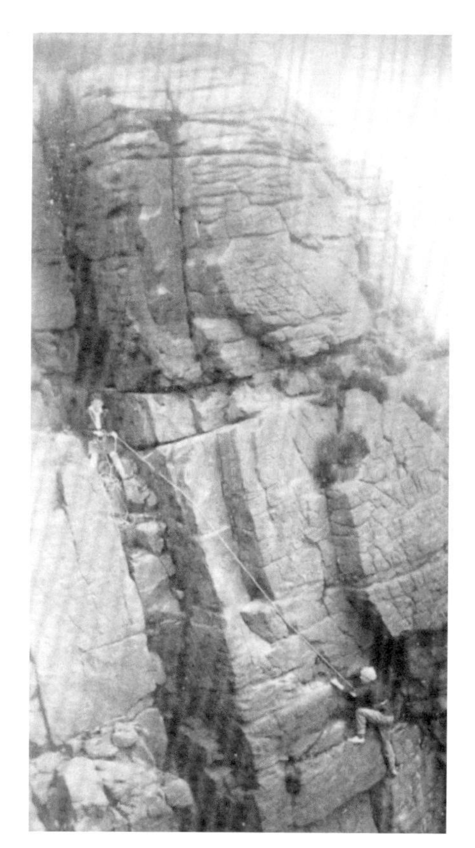

Above left: Long Climb, a classic climbing route on the remote gritstone edge of Laddow Rocks and scene of the accident in 1928 whereby Edgar Pryor was knocked from his stance and received severe injuries. This single event is celebrated as the point at which it was realised that some form of special equipment was necessary to deal with injuries in the hills.

Above right: Long Climb is a 35m route graded as Hard Very Difficult, but its popularity has made some of the key holds rather polished.

A group of ramblers peruse the map that in the 1930s–40s would probably have used the 1in to the mile scale and possibly have been printed on canvas. The now familiar 1:25000 (2½in to 1 mile) with the metric grid system was not introduced until 1945 and early editions were comparatively expensive.

Bill Thompson, the first team leader of Sett Valley MRT, shows off the Thomas stretcher, probably from the rescue post at Reservoir House, Hayfield.

A Mountain Rescue Committee Rescue Post. The plaque was designed for the MRC by Wilfred Wood in 1954. The first design depicted a red cross but the British Red Cross objected stating that use of the cross was limited by the Geneva Convention. This new design of a white cross on a red background was acceptable and became a very familiar sight across the country, attached to various buildings on the approach routes to the hills.

locations for free use by anyone attempting to assist a casualty in the hills. These kit stores were to become known as 'Rescue Posts' and each one was to be sponsored by a climbing club.

The Fell and Rock Climbing Club undertook to provide and maintain several posts in the Lake District and the Scottish Mountaineering Club agreed to a few more in Scotland. In Wales the Rucksack Club provided a post at its hut at Tal y Braich that was later moved to Idwal Cottage. The Climbers' Club maintained a kit at Helyg and the Midland Association of Mountaineers another in the Snowdonia area.

The initial few led the way and very soon other clubs were accepting responsibility for providing and maintaining posts in their areas. As the interest in providing posts grew, a more permanent committee structure was needed to handle the funds and deal with the administration of equipment supply. A new committee was formed which met for the first time in September 1936 and was known as 'The First Aid Committee of British Mountaineering Clubs'. Most of the original stretcher committee members served in the new administration and were joined by representatives of six other mountaineering clubs. As the new committee got itself organised representatives from the Youth Hostel Association, the Ramblers' Association and some university clubs were asked to represent wider walking and outdoor interests.

The MRC Rescue Post plaque at Hooks Car, the popular end of Stanage Edge and scene of many climbing accidents. The sign directs a would-be rescuer to Rescue Post 40 at Hollin Bank, Ranger Briefing Centre, about 500m away. The briefing centre was not regularly manned and access to the rescue equipment meant breaking a glass key case.

As teams became established and bought their own equipment the use of rescue posts declined. Theft and vandalism also took their toll so the posts were becoming very expensive to maintain. In 1989 the MRC, in an effort to reduce vandalism, asked the Ordnance Survey not to depict the post on future reprints of maps.

Concern was also being voiced that it was better for the casualty's interests if a rescue team attended to an incident rather than encouraging others, with no experience of first aid or rescue, to deal with the situation. It was this basic theory that eventually led the MRC to stop publishing the list of posts in its own handbook after 1992. The final demise of the rescue posts came in 1993 when the MRC decided not to make further supplies of equipment available to posts. The MRC's original objective of providing rescue equipment for use by anyone had been overturned in favour of helping the rescue teams provide the service. It was a momentous decision and a major landmark in the history of mountain rescue.

THE 1940s AND WARTIME

The war years brought further casualties to the hills and mountains of Britain, but these were not walkers and climbers out for recreation but the pilots and aircrew of British, Allied and enemy aircraft. Navigation systems in most aircraft were primitive and relied mainly on the ability of the crew to recognise landmarks from the air. Mountainous areas attract their own weather systems and are frequently plagued by fog and cloud, making observation of the ground difficult, if not impossible. Disorientated aircrew often thought they were flying over much lower ground than they actually were and the result was all too often the sudden impact of the aircraft with the ground. The crews had little chance of escape and the rescue of any survivors was often dependent on the crash having been witnessed by someone on the ground. In remote areas with bad visibility crash sites are surprisingly difficult to locate. The high moors and crags of the Peak District claimed their share and over 250 aircraft crashes are recorded in the area. The recovery of the wartime crews became the responsibility of the RAF 28 Maintenance Unit based at Harpur Hill near Buxton.

There are over 250 known aircraft wrecks in and around the Peak District, mostly from the war years. The chances of the crew surviving the initial crash were slim but if they did they would have to wait for the team from RAF Harpur Hill in Buxton to be alerted. Most of the wreckage would have been removed or burnt shortly after the crash. Time and weather have taken their toll so finding what little wreckage remains today is a challenge.

RAF Harpur Hill's team members liaise with the police during the search for two RAF Gloster Meteor aircraft which crashed into Slidden's Moss near Black Hill in April 1951. Both pilots were killed in the accident.

RAF team members at the impact site of a United States Air Force RB-29A which crashed at Higher Shelf Stones on Bleaklow Moor on 3 November 1948. Despite the rescue team being on site very quickly it was too late to help any of the thirteen crew members.

In 1942 the base Medical Officer was Flight Lieutenant David 'Doc' Crichton who, although knowing little about mountaineering, became involved simply from a need to respond to the calls that were coming in about crashed aircraft. As the numbers of calls increased, 'Doc' Crichton slowly started to gather together a small band of volunteers to help. Available equipment was basic, mainly a standard RAF issue medical kit and a stretcher, so the unit started to design its own stretcher using parts from a bed as runners.

All mountain rescue activity in the RAF at the time was unofficial but the work carried out at Harpur Hill and several other units around the country led to formal recognition in January 1944, after it was revealed in a report that 517 airmen had lost their lives in mountainous areas of Britain. By the time the Harpur Hill unit was officially recognised it had already dealt with over forty incidents, and Flight Lieutenant Crichton was awarded the MBE in 1946 for his services to mountain rescue over the previous three years. 'Doc' Crichton left Harpur Hill in the same year and eventually retired from the RAF with the rank of Air Commodore.

The Harpur Hill unit continued its work after the war and was kept reasonably busy with aviation incidents throughout the 1950s. The team also assisted the police with many civilian incidents and was the only organised search and rescue resource available until the Peak Park Planning Board started to become more actively involved in the mid-1950s.

A memorable incident occurred in March 1959 when the unit was called to its first underground rescue. At 3.30 p.m. on Sunday 22 Neil Moss and several other experienced cavers had entered Peak Cavern in Castleton to explore a recently discovered shaft some distance beyond the public show cavern. Neil became trapped in a very narrow passage and his companions were unable to free him. The local civilian cave rescue team attempted a recovery but were also unable to make any headway. At 2.00 a.m. on Monday the RAF at Harpur Hill were asked if they could assist. Carbon dioxide poisoning brought on by the use of carbide lamps had caused Moss to lose consciousness soon after becoming trapped. For two days the civilian and RAF teams worked together to free the Oxford undergraduate but all was in vain and he died where he was. Still

The RAF Stafford Team. After the closure of RAF Harpur Hill the rescue team was transferred to Stafford.

the body could not be freed for recovery and the Home Office finally gave permission for it to be sealed in and entombed forever.

For a short time following this incident, and until the unit transferred to RAF Stafford, the Harpur Hill unit maintained a small amount of cave rescue equipment. Derbyshire Cave Rescue Organisation learnt a lot from the rescue in both administrative and technical procedures and the incident probably gave birth to the modern and greatly respected team of today.

The Harpur Hill RAF Maintenance Unit closed in 1959 and the rescue team transferred its base to RAF Stafford from where it continued to serve the Peak District. The unit finally closed in 2005 and the responsibility for its operational area was divided between RAF Valley, Anglesey, and RAF Leeming, North Yorkshire.

POST-WAR CONFUSION

Following the war the number of visitors to the Peak District increased dramatically and the featureless peaty plateaux seemed to draw people from far and near. The majority of the Peak moors were in private ownership and access was legally restricted, but that did not put off the determined hiker and climber. However, it naturally follows that footpaths were far less distinct than today and only a few had signposts or way-markers. Getting lost was a real hazard!

In today's world of instant communications and rapid transport it is sometimes difficult to imagine the difficulties that a mountain accident or report of a missing person in a remote area could cause. Just getting word off the hill to raise the alarm may have taken hours and then the problems of organising a suitable response could take even longer. The police were, and still are, the responsible authority, but even they had primitive communications by today's standards. In the Peak District, before the mid-1950s, there was no central organisation to which the police could turn for the specialist help required and they had instead to make the best use they could of their own local knowledge and contacts. However, mountain rescue was beginning to organise itself in other parts of the country and the Peak District would play its part in the development. The densely populated North Midlands was the home of many of the established climbing clubs that were instrumental in developing the rescue service. Many of the names now credited in rescue circles as being the forefathers of the service came from the Manchester area and most would have had a sound experience of the Peak's moors and moody weather.

1946: THE MOUNTAIN RESCUE COMMITTEE

In 1946, after the end of the war, the increase in outdoor activities and the broadening responsibilities of the First Aid Committee prompted the members to take ownership of all the equipment kept at the rescue posts. To reflect its changing character and functions the committee also decided to change its name to the Mountain Rescue Committee (MRC).

In 1938 the First Aid Committee published its first handbook, which was prepared by Alfred Pigott and simply listed the twelve rescue posts which had then been established. In 1946 the Mountain Rescue Committee produced a new handbook based on information supplied to J.E.Q. Barford, the first secretary of the British Mountaineering Council, for an appropriate chapter in his book, *Climbing in Britain*, published by Penguin Books. The new handbook, entitled *Mountain Rescue and First Aid*, was printed in 1947, selling for 4*d* (slightly less than 2p) per copy. The booklet gave hints and tips on what to do in an emergency and how to administer first aid. The rescue posts were listed as were details of how to send messages for help and who to inform if equipment required repair or replenishment.

Amendments to the booklet were regularly published, but a completely new handbook entitled *Mountain and Cave Rescue* appeared in 1956, prepared by Jack Caldwell, a Mountain Rescue Committee member and Rucksack Club treasurer. This book was designed for consumption by the general public and for use as a basic text for those taking courses at mountaineering centres. This handbook was the first of an annual publication that grew in size over the years as the number of posts increased and rescue teams and their parent regions were formed. Caldwell continued to produce the handbook for eighteen years until his retirement

The emphasis was still on providing rescue post equipment for use by anyone. Civilian rescue teams were still an *ad hoc* assembly of those available to assist at the time of an accident and often consisted of the local policeman, farmers and anyone staying temporarily in the nearest climbing hut. Each rescue post had a nominated supervisor to look after it and it was often that person who would lead the rescue attempt. Some local people were therefore becoming regularly involved with rescue simply because they were always in the right place at the right time. They began to realise the benefit of having a group of people who knew each other's abilities, had good local knowledge, outdoor experience and suitable clothing. So it was that rescue teams began to form in various parts of the country; the first formal civilian rescue teams are credited to be Coniston MRT, founded in 1946 under the leadership of Jim Cameron, and Keswick MRT, founded by Colonel 'Rusty' Westmorland in 1947.

1949: WILSON HEY AND MORPHIA

Serving on the Mountain Rescue Committee from its inception was Mr Wilson H. Hey, president of the Rucksack Club and later to become president of the Manchester Medical Society. From 1934 he actively fought for the right to supply morphia to rescue posts.

His first application to the Home Office was turned down, presumably because rescue posts were not very secure sites and were open for anyone to use them. Hey, however, continued to supply the very active posts and applied again to the Home Office in 1949, freely admitting that the drug had been used over fifty times in the past twenty years. A Home Office inspector was sent to meet with Hey but an argument developed and Hey refused to show the inspector his drug register. In October that year Hey was prosecuted and fined £10 with £10 costs, a lot of money in 1949.

Hey was undeterred and arranged another meeting with the Home Office but this time he was accompanied by many leading and well-known medical names of the time, some with Everest and other alpine experience. In December 1949 the Home Office relented under the pressure and permitted the supply of morphia to rescue posts, subject to close supervision. Since that time all teams have been able to obtain and administer a limited range of analgesics in a very controlled and documented manner. It has been a privilege that the teams have respected by adhering closely to the regulations and one that has been appreciated by hundreds of injured walkers and climbers over the last sixty years.

The Rescue Post network was still the backbone of the rescue system and there was a great emphasis on self-help. The 1947 MRC Handbook lists a total of sixteen posts in England and Wales, with just three first-aid posts in Derbyshire. These were at Hope, under the watchful eye of Dr W. Baillie, Tunstead House, Kinder, supervised by Mr S. Forrester, and The Rifle Range at Crowden, supervised by Mrs E. Fazakerley. No rescue teams are mentioned.

By 1957 the handbook for England and Wales listed a total of thirty-five first-aid posts and ten rescue teams, four of which were RAF units. In the Peak District a new post had been added

A group of ramblers leaves Hayfield and heads up the Kinder Valley towards the plateau. Walking in groups helped share the cost of maps and transport and meant that assistance was readily at hand in the event of an accident.

The first emblem of the Peak District National Park depicts the 900-year-old Peveril Castle which stands above Castleton.

at the Nag's Head, Edale, under the supervision of landlord Fred Heardman, and three teams were also listed, these being Derbyshire Cave Rescue, Edale Rescue Team and RAF Harpur Hill, Buxton.

1949: NATIONAL PARKS ACT

The story of the fight for access to the moors is well documented and it suffices to say that the pressure from the clubs, outdoor enthusiasts and many others finally brought about the National Parks and Access to Countryside Act of 1949. From this legislation the first of the country's national parks, The Peak District National Park, was born in April 1951. Within two years the Peak Park Planning Board negotiated two agreements to be signed with the landowners, giving ramblers and climbers the right of access to large parts of Kinder Scout, including the highest point in the Peak District. Other access agreements followed, including a significant thirty-one square miles of Bleaklow in 1954 and a further fourteen square miles of the moor in 1957.

A strategic component of the access agreements was the provision of a warden service to patrol the areas and enforce the bylaws. The inauguration of the Peak District National Park Warden Service (now Ranger Service) took place outside the Nag's Head pub in Edale in 1954. Present at the proceedings was the then seventy-seven-year-old G.H.B. Ward, the individual who, in 1900, had invited walkers to join him and start the Sheffield Clarion Club. A number of volunteers had been recruited from the local mountaineering and rambling clubs to assist with patrolling the moors at weekends to ensure the access bylaws were being upheld. The first full-time head warden was Tom Tomlinson, who features later in this book as one who helped co-ordinate many searches on Kinder and Bleaklow. He had previously been warden of the Edale Youth Hostel for ten years. He, his two full-time assistants and some of the weekend volunteer wardens would soon play a significant part in the formal setting up of the Peak District Mountain Rescue Organisation.

1955: THE PEAK PARK PLANNING BOARD ACCESS AND FOOTPATHS SUB-COMMITTEE

As the Peak Park Planning Board (PPPB) began to negotiate with landowners for more land with open access for the public, the number of incidents began to increase. Fred Heardman was the licensee of the Nag's Head pub in Edale, which also served as an Information Centre for the National Park, and consequently it was often Fred who would first hear of an accident on the

One of the first voluntary Peak Park Planning Board wardens, a well-dressed lady in tweeds, showing the green and red armband that they then wore.

moor and he was regularly leading small groups of volunteers to effect a rescue. Tom Tomlinson, as Head Warden for the National Park, was also being contacted and it was he who convinced the Board that rescue equipment should be provided at Edale.

John Foster was the Planning Officer for the PPPB when it was affiliated with the MRC in mid-1955 and sponsored a Thomas Stretcher and first-aid equipment to be maintained at the Nag's Head. The equipment was in regular use from the very start, for example in the rescue of Mr Fernihough, a resident of Sheffield and a member of the Pennine Mountaineering Club, who fell 24ft whilst leading a rock climb on Upper Tor in Grindsbrook, Edale. The new stretcher was brought up from Edale and Mr Fernihough, who had suffered a fractured pelvis, was carried back down the valley by his club mates and some PPPB voluntary wardens.

THE VOLUNTARY WARDEN SEARCH AND RESCUE ORGANISATION.

In March of the same year Fred Heardman was asked to attempt to recruit volunteers from the clubs and organisations who had helped to form the PPPB voluntary wardens. He was successful in getting between fifty and sixty names of those who were already weekend voluntary wardens and were willing to be called out in the event of a missing person report. A shorter list was drawn up of more local volunteers who could offer their assistance at the time of an accident.

A meeting was planned for the morning of Sunday 19 February 1956 to discuss the proposed 'Voluntary Warden Search and Rescue Organisation' which was to be followed by a demonstration and exercise at the head of Grindsbrook, Edale. Mr Wilson Hey, then chairman of the Mountain Rescue Committee of England and Wales was invited to the meeting, to be held in Cooper's Café at Edale, but, unfortunately, his health deteriorated suddenly and he died before the meeting. Mr Noel Kirkman, who was to succeed Hey as chairman, attended instead along with Mr A.S. (Fred) Pigott, also of the Mountain Rescue Committee, who was able to show a ciné film on mountain rescue techniques in North Wales.

Representatives from Derbyshire Police attended, bringing a Duff Stretcher from Glossop Police Station. From the Derbyshire Fire Service, Divisional Officer Reader (Buxton) and Station Officer Smith (Glossop) attended the exercise along with five firemen with a Neil Robertson Stretcher. Members of RAF Harpur Hill were also present and gave a demonstration of their skills. A total of 130 people took part in the afternoon exercise, which involved splitting into three groups to test the different stretchers. The police took their Duff Stretcher up the steep scree slope of Foxholes whilst the fire service carried their Neil Robertson into Dry Gully. The Thomas Stretcher from the Edale post went up via Golden Clough carried by the wardens. All three stretcher parties met up at Four Jacks Cabin and the evacuation of mock casualties began at three-minute intervals. The ground was icy and it was agreed by all that the broad runners of the Thomas Stretcher had won the day. The meeting and the exercise were declared a success and the 'Voluntary Wardens' team was born.

Another meeting was planned for May and, by then, a call-out system had been devised using a 'Convenor' in each of the major towns surrounding the park who could be contacted by telephone and who could then call out the volunteers in his neighbourhood. This meeting was also held in Cooper's Café and was led by Philip Daley as chairman of the Access and Paths Sub-committee of the PPPB. It was generally agreed that the existing arrangements put in place by Heardman were adequate for weekday accidents. Local volunteers could also cover accidents at the weekend with their numbers supplemented by other Voluntary Wardens in the Hope Valley.

The call-out system for the remainder of the organisation, in the event of a search, was then discussed and convenors were appointed for Manchester, Rotherham, Chesterfield, Doncaster, Sheffield and Hope. The system had several problems, a major one being communication as it was reported that many of the volunteers did not have telephones and could only be contacted when at work. Another problem was that of transport, for few members had their own cars. A list was compiled of who could and who could not provide transport and local pick-up points were agreed. Fred Heardman also commented that, as most of these volunteers would only be called for a search, speed was not too important and it would therefore be quite satisfactory if they made their way by train. The PPPB also agreed to provide six whistles!

Although not actually at the meeting, Geoffrey Sutton, warden of White Hall Open Country Pursuits Centre at Buxton, had stated by letter that he would be able to provide a contingent of quality rock climbers in the event of an incident. He also volunteered the services of his wife, as she was a good mountaineer and a doctor. A Land Rover and a van would also be available from the centre if required.

Left: Fred Heardman in 1954, outside his pub, The Nag's Head at Edale, directing visitors towards Kinder Scout via Grindsbrook, soon to become the start of the Pennine Way. Standing to the right is Tom Tomlinson, the first head warden of the National Park.

Below: Tom Tomlinson leads the first group of voluntary wardens on a patrol on Good Friday in 1954.

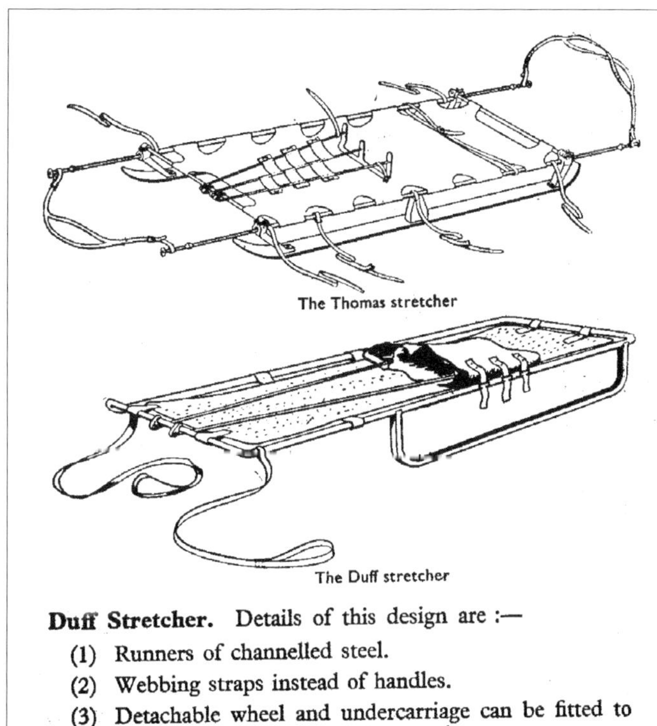
The Thomas stretcher

The Duff stretcher

Duff Stretcher. Details of this design are :—

(1) Runners of channelled steel.

(2) Webbing straps instead of handles.

(3) Detachable wheel and undercarriage can be fitted to the runners for moving along paths.

A page from the Mountain Rescue Committee Handbook of 1957 showing comparable diagrams of the Duff and Thomas stretchers which could be found in Rescue Posts.

The Voluntary Warden Search and Rescue Organisation was taking shape and was boosted by an offer from Derbyshire Fire Service to provide a crew of five personnel, suitably clothed and equipped, to undertake mountain rescue work. The Fire Service also purchased a Vary Pistol for use by the organisation to signal to rescue parties on the hill. The use of 'walkie-talkies' had been dismissed as being impractical.

Fred Heardman and Tom Tomlinson, between them, had a busy time organising several rescue incidents during the remainder of 1956 and through 1957, and the rescue equipment maintained at the Nag's Head was in regular use. These are just some of those incidents:

On the 4th November 1956 an 11-year-old boy is reported to have slipped on the steep rough slope of Jacob's Ladder near Upper Booth and suffered a fractured arm. The lad was tended to by the Edale doctor, Dr Lafferty, before being taken to Manchester Royal Infirmary by the Bakewell ambulance.

A woman is reported to have dislocated her knee whilst walking on Kinder Scout on the 11th November. Voluntary wardens tended to her injuries and she was carried by stretcher down to Edale. Again Dr Lafferty attended this incident, which took over three hours to complete.

On the evening of Boxing Day 1956 a major search was organised for two members of a party of four students from Manchester missing on Kinder. The four were members of the Black and Tan Climbing Club and had left the Snake Inn at 1.00pm. They ignored advice that the prevailing weather conditions made it unsafe to venture on to Kinder Scout but instead set off into the snow and wind. At 8.45 that night two of the party returned to the Snake Inn to report that their friends were lost in deep snow on the moors. The police were informed but road conditions made it difficult to travel along the Snake Pass. The search party therefore was made up mainly of other members of the students' Black and Tan Climbing Club. The couple was found about 3.00am, cold and tired, and were taken back down to the Snake Inn.

The following Saturday a 39 year old woman became separated from her party of skiers on Featherbed Moss. The woman had stopped to tend to her dog and when she looked round the rest of the party had gone. The weather was such that ski tracks were quickly covered and the woman became disorientated. The search was launched at 5.00pm, with search parties coming from Glossop Police Station and Glossop Fire Station. RAF Harpur Hill MRT was called out and additional search parties from Barnsley Mountaineering Club, Chesterfield Rambler's Association and Glossop Rambling Club were also brought in. Tom Tomlinson was also waiting for instructions and standing by at Edale with another search party. The whole operation was controlled by the police using the AA box near to the Snake Pass summit. Unfortunately the event nearly ended in tragedy when rescuer Harold Swift, a 38-year-old member of the Barnsley club and a Volunteer Warden, fell down a deep gully quite close to the Snake Pass road. He suffered severe shoulder and back injuries in the fall and had to be given first aid treatment on site by members of the RAF team. A stretcher was brought in and the police and members of Glossop Rambling Club managed to drag the casualty back up the 50-feet-deep gully to the road. Mr Swift was taken to Ashton District Infirmary where he was detained for two weeks. The woman later walked in to the Snake Inn about 11.00pm, apparently unharmed and accompanied by her dog.

A serious incident occurred on Sunday 17 February 1957 when 14-year-old Boy Scout, Michael Parsons, fell from the top of Kinder Downfall. Michael was part of a group from St Catherine's Scout Unit, Didsbury, Manchester, and had been seen standing close to the edge. The weather was thick with mist and, although the Scout Master heard Michael's scream, despite an extensive search in the poor conditions they couldn't find the lad. The party intended to make its way off to Hayfield but got lost and ended up on the A57 Snake Pass road some five hours after the accident. Heardman and Tomlinson were contacted in the early hours of Monday and they in turn called RAF Harpur Hill MRT. It was 5.00am when the rescuers found Michael on a ledge about fifty feet from the top of the Downfall. He had suffered face and leg injuries and was deeply hypothermic. The RAF team and other volunteers carried the stretcher down to Hayfield Reservoir where the RAF medic examined the boy's injuries before he was taken to Stockport Infirmary. Despite having suffered injuries in the fall and endured twelve hours in freezing weather the lad made a full recovery; a notable success for the rescue service.

The same night two other scouts were missing on the moor but they were able to walk off to Hayfield in the early hours. Unfortunately they did not tell the police they were safe until they got home to Stockport and the search for them went on until 9.00am before it was called off.

In June 1957 two more incidents are recorded at Hayfield where the Voluntary Wardens used the rescue post equipment from Reservoir House. Both incidents involved girls with lower leg injuries.

Messrs Heardman and Tomlinson were out again on the night of June 10th following the report of another scout who had become separated from his party. At midnight the message went out to the Conveners to call a small team together for an overnight search and a party of

The moors still present a hazard to aircraft as this helicopter crash site near to Ashop Head Rocks, Kinder Scout demonstrates. On 24 October 1997 this Bell Jet-Ranger operated by Yorkshire Helicopters was working for the National Trust airlifting stone for footpath repairs on Kinder Scout.

> nineteen rescuers met at Edale. They searched through the night without success and at 6.00am preparations for a full-scale search of the moor were being made ready. However, the youth had walked through the night and had stumbled on two men camping near Kinder Downfall. The men looked after the scout for the remainder of the night and then they all made their way down to Hayfield in the morning.

This was one of a number of incidents involving scouts or cadets, and highlighted a growing problem of the moors being used for endurance training rather than recreation. Fred Heardman was also very critical of the standard of dress and the equipment that many of these youth groups were carrying. He highlighted that the scout who had fallen from the Downfall in February was only wearing shorts, wellington boots and a plastic cape! The PPPB took the matter seriously and arranged a meeting in September 1957 with Clive Bembrose, the County Commissioner for Derbyshire Boy Scouts. Also present at the meeting were A. Rimmer, County Secretary, and Major Hewitt, Field Commissioner. On behalf of the board, John Foster outlined the number of incidents that had recently occurred involving scouts and the apparent inadequacies in their kit. It was agreed that any scout group coming to the Peak District would be asked to contact the Head Warden, giving him the opportunity to offer a short talk on safety on Kinder. The scouting chiefs made note of the recommended clothing and equipment standards for walking on the moors and promised to circulate the details to all the scouts in Derbyshire and neighbouring counties. The PPPB also offered to consider providing a proficiency badge to encourage scouts to get involved with the work of the park wardens.

RAF Harpur Hill was also still very active and it was this unit that was called to deal with the crash of a Miles Hawk Trainer, a small light aircraft, at Kinder Low on 28 July 1957. Mr William Hall, an ex-RAF wartime pilot had left Blackpool for the short trip to Manchester's Barton Airfield. Exactly why the aircraft was approaching Kinder Scout has never been established but a local farmer saw it flying just below cloud level when it suddenly banked and disappeared into the mist. Moments later the sound of the crash was heard. The alarm was raised and the RAF team was called out, but there was no hope for the pilot who was killed on impact.

Since the establishment of the Voluntary Warden Search and Rescue Organisation the subject of insurance had been a thorny issue and an accident to rescuer Mr Swift on Boxing Day 1956 concentrated minds. The PPPB had arranged insurance for its staff for Saturdays, Sundays and

Tom Stephenson, Ewan MacColl and Fred Heardman stand at the head of Grindsbrook and reflect on the story of the fight for access to the private grouse moors of the Peak District. Tom Stephenson was a lifelong campaigner for the right to roam and was also responsible for creating the Pennine Way in 1965, Britain's first long distance footpath which started at Edale. Folk singer Ewan MacColl made the right to roam campaign famous with his song *The Manchester Rambler*.

holidays but there was no cover for weekdays or for any of the risks of rock climbing. However, the increase in the Voluntary Warden establishment and its by now official exposure to the risks involved in mountain rescue called for a review. The PPPB had already been seeking advice from several other bodies and a letter to Tom Stephenson, secretary of the Ramblers' Association, suggested a company in Manchester, which would finally provide the policy.

When considering various quotations and policies, a clerk of the PPPB is quoted as making the following reassuring comment, 'I don't think we need be concerned with the payment of death benefits, the chief risk to persons on rescue operations appears to be from possible injuries.' Insurance cover was agreed in September 1957 with Keith Shipton & Co. of Spring Gardens, Manchester, and underwritten by Lloyds. The PPPB agreed to pay the sum of £12 10*s* premium to cover its volunteers for up to £1,000 on death or £10 per week for total disablement. It was emphasised that the cover was only available when the volunteers were acting under the Head Warden's instruction in a search and rescue situation.

Word about the insurance policy became more widely known and in 1959 the Mountain Rescue Committee asked for details as it was considering a similar scheme for all members of its affiliated teams. The Lake District National Park also requested details as it too was looking at the liabilities of its wardens when involved in rescue work. By August that year a new national policy had been agreed between the MRC and Keith Shipton & Co. that covered everyone involved in mountain rescue anywhere in Great Britain or Ireland, providing they were using equipment

A casualty being carried down the sides of Grindsbrook on a Thomas stretcher in the 1970s.

supplied by an MRC affiliated team or body. The premium was £100 per annum and the MRC asked the PPPB to cease its own policy and pool its money into the national policy. The PPPB agreed and the new cover started from 1 September with the additional financial support from the Lake District and Snowdonia national parks. No claim was made on this policy for ten years until, on 15 June 1969, a tragic accident occurred in Birkness Combe at Buttermere in the Lake District, where two members of Cockermouth Mountain Rescue Team were killed. The insurance company paid out but the following renewal terms were unacceptable. Representations were made to the Association of Chief Police Officers asking local Chief Constables to provide insurance for teams within their area. Support from Lord Hunt and the then Prime Minister, Jim Callaghan, finally persuaded the Home Office in 1972 to agree that Chief Constables may use their discretion and provide insurance where they thought appropriate. Since that date the Association of Chief Police Officers has been represented on the Mountain Rescue Council and appropriately the first delegate was Walter Stansfield, Chief Constable of Derbyshire.

As the moors in the Peak District became more popular the number of reported incidents increased and the warden service was kept busy. Two separate accidents occurred on Jacob's Ladder in October 1958, both involving youth groups. A Sea Scout broke an arm and a young girl broke a leg whilst descending the steep shale bank. On 1 December another scout was involved in an accident reported to be near Crowden Head in the centre of the Kinder plateau. Tom Tomlinson led a number of wardens to this incident site finally located at Kinder Gates and a three-hour carry-off commenced. The youth had fallen from a frozen peat hag and had broken a bone in his left ankle.

Sunday 22 March 1959 posed a technical problem for the six volunteer PPPB wardens who were patrolling around the Kinder Downfall area. A young boy had slipped from the crag on the south side of the waterfall and had fallen about 80ft onto a narrow ledge. Four local climbers had already attempted to help the youth who had sustained nasty head and facial injuries. The downward sloping ledge was about another 80ft from the ground and the climbers built a makeshift wall on the ledge to prevent the youth falling any further. The rescue post equipment was sent for from Kinder Reservoir House, Hayfield, and the police and ambulance were informed. A stretcher was eventually lowered to the ledge, and, with the boy securely fastened in, it was hoisted back to the top. It was reported as a difficult operation in poor weather and swirling mist but there appears to be no record of whether the boy recovered. It was following this incident that the Peak Park Planning Board purchased two hemp ropes, at a total cost of £5, to be kept at the Reservoir House Rescue Post, which until this time had only a stretcher and a first-aid rucksack.

The first record of morphia having been used at a rescue in the Peak District was during an incident in Grindsbrook on Easter Monday 1959 when a fifteen-year-old girl slipped on a steep slope and hurt her thigh and knee. The injuries were obviously painful and the Edale doctor, Dr Wilkinson, was asked to attend. Morphia had technically been available to rescue posts since 1949 but no record can be found of exactly when it was first kept at Edale. The unfortunate girl was brought down on a stretcher before being taken to Stockport Infirmary. Also on Easter Monday a boy slipped on the rocks in Grindsbrook and caused injury to his back. The report tells of the stretcher being brought from the rescue post at Edale and the rescue being 'commendably handled by wardens and carried out in good time using the Board's equipment'.

Morphia is again recorded as having been used on 2 April when a twenty-four-year-old woman suffered a compound leg fracture whilst jumping over peat groughs on Kinder plateau. This time it was Dr Lafferty who accompanied the rescue party back onto the moor where morphia was administered.

Fred Heardman had attended all of the three incidents and reported to the Board that, in every case, the casualties were wearing 'unsuitable footwear'!

The number of incidents being reported on Kinder prompted Bill Thompson of New Mills to write to the PPPB in June 1959 suggesting the provision of a rescue equipment box adjacent to Kinder Downfall. He further suggested the provision of a telephone link from the Downfall to the Reservoir House Rescue Post. The Board responded by letter stating that the provision of rescue equipment at posts was the responsibility of the MRC and it was doubted that the Board would sanction such expenditure without support from the MRC. No mention was made in the return letter about a telephone link and the subject appears to have been forgotten.

Whilst the local wardens and volunteers had been relatively busy with rescue incidents through the late 1950s, the full strength of the 'Convenor' system of calling out extra people for an extended search had not been tested in reality. Several training exercises had been held and each was relatively well attended, but the initial enthusiasm that was inspired when the system was set up was waning. There were originally seven convenors but the number had dropped to four and it was noted that not all the volunteers were being contacted and told of a forthcoming exercise. Two of the four remaining convenors were said to be heavily committed to other duties and replacements for them had not come forward. Furthermore, both Heardman and Thompson were beginning to have their doubts about the effective control of long lines of sweep searchers; smaller groups of people that knew each other had proved to be more successful.

The PPPB Access and Paths Sub-committee, which oversaw the search and rescue organisation, held a meeting in November 1959 at which some of these concerns were raised. The warden's rescue unit was working well and coping admirably with daytime accidents, both at the weekend and during the week. However, the committee concluded that the present system for calling out searchers was no longer viable and that it would fail if it were activated in an emergency. Other recent developments were also considered. The Board had received several approaches from clubs connected to the voluntary warden service asking for the facilities to carry out their own practice rescue exercises. As a result two new search and rescue groups had been formed, one at Glossop and one at New Mills. It was thought that as many as fifty people could be assembled for a search, using these two teams and the wardens. Additional searchers would also still be available from White Hall Open Country Pursuits Centre at Buxton and from the RAF team at Harpur Hill.

A Thomas stretcher being used to carry a casualty down the hill. The patient is wrapped in an MRC casualty bag, similar to a sleeping bag but made from robust material and with a full-length zip for easy access. The bags were originally filled with duck down but the modern bag is lined with thick fibre-pile which gives an instant feeling of warmth.

Police and rescuers survey the wreck of a de Havilland Rapide which crashed onto Kinder on 30 December 1963. The aircraft was on a course from Teesside to Birmingham but concerns over fuel caused an unplanned diversion into Manchester. Strong winds and poor visibility made flying the elderly aeroplane difficult and the aircraft struck the moor and disintegrated. Both crew survived but were severely injured and as there had been no time to send a distress message they had to wait for help. The wreckage was spotted by a searching helicopter just before darkness fell but because of the extreme weather it was unable to land. A rescue team from Edale eventually helped the casualties to safety.

CADETS JOIN THE SEARCH

Members of Royton A.T.C. Mountain Rescue Squad have joined police in a search for 12-year-old John Kilbride, of Ashton-under-Lyne, led by their commanding officer, Squadron Leader R. Kenworth. The cadets are seen with police doghandler R. Spencer, of Leigh.

Squadron Leader Bob Kenworthy leads the Royton ATC MRT whilst assisting in the search for twelve-year-old John Kilbride, a victim of Brady and Hindley, the Moors Murderers.

The committee resolved to discontinue the convenor system and instead encourage local clubs to train their own members in search techniques. It was also thought that, as the members of these groups would know each other, they would work together more effectively and would have a better method of contacting each other in the event of a reported missing person. Each club that agreed to train its members would therefore be asked to appoint one person who could be telephoned by the Board if their services were required. The committee finally concluded that if even larger numbers of searchers were needed then an appeal for help could be made via the BBC.

The door was now open for the formation of rescue teams and there were to be many that would take up the challenge in one form or another. The Peak Park Planning Board retained the responsibility for calling the teams but a short period of confusion was to follow. 1959 was also the year in which the RAF station at Harpur Hill in Buxton closed. The rescue team moved to RAF Stafford and, whilst the team would still be active in the area, the new base was some considerable distance from the Peak and the team's effectiveness for dealing with emergencies was reduced.

THREE

THE 1960S AND SEVEN DEATHS

In the early 1960s there were several teams becoming established in and around the area and the Peak District National Park Warden Service, which formed in 1954, had also become a very useful resource. Some of the teams had evolved from Venture Scout Units so any lack of experience was made up for by energy and enthusiasm. However, training, equipment and, above all, co-ordination were lacking and three events in the early 1960s were to prove the case.

In all the three incidents, local volunteers, police, and even the RAF, did their best under the circumstances, and it is only with hindsight that the failings of the system can be seen. The authors of this book do not offer any criticism of those involved; indeed the courage and endurance of those young people who went onto the hills in such adverse conditions can only be admired and praised. It is likely that the people who died in these incidents succumbed to the weather before any of the rescue teams knew of the situation. With today's weather forecasting, our greater understanding of hypothermia and with modern-day clothing, maybe some would have survived long enough for help to arrive.

1962: GLOSSOP CHILDREN LOST ON THE MOORS. TWO DIE

Late on the evening of Tuesday 18 December 1962 two young children were reported missing from home in Glossop. The children were brother and sister, aged seven and eleven years old, and had last been seen by their mother about lunchtime in the town centre. The police organised a major search of the town, which later started to take in some of the open ground and the moors surrounding Glossop. The children were not to be found until four days later when a fourteen-year-old scout, a member of a search team from Sheffield, located two bodies on open moorland at Featherbed Moss. He and his other scout friends returned to the Snake Road and waved down a car for a lift back into Glossop in order to report their find to the police.

The search had been difficult due to the lack of information, and bad weather had hampered the moorland sweeps. With no formal organisation to call upon the search parties were made up from all sorts of organisations that heard of the incident on the BBC radio service. The groups included eighty police and police cadets from Derbyshire, units from RAF Stafford Mountain Rescue Team and RAF Hemswell, New Mills Mountain Rescue Team under the leadership of Mr W. Thompson and Glossop Rover Scout Mountain Rescue Team under the leadership of Mr R. Davies. Also involved were 195 school children from the local grammar school, several scout groups from Sheffield, Stockport and Cheshire, a party from Glossop Peak Camping and Climbing Club, the Manchester Ramblers' Association, and groups from Sheffield Climbing and Caving Club and Macclesfield Caving Club. Fourteen members of the Civil Defence had volunteered to assist and brought with them two 'walkie-talkie' radios. Had the search continued then George Garlick, Fred Heardman and Tom Tomlinson from the National Park Warden Service were preparing to meet ramblers off the trains from Sheffield and Manchester in order to persuade them to assist in a full search of Kinder Scout, but in the event they were not required.

OLDHAM EVENING CHRONICLE, Monday, January 21, 1963. 9

Two climbers swept to death in Chew Valley

ALMOST 24 hours after the rescue operation swung into action, the bodies of two climbers swept from a rock face by an avalanche in Chew Valley, Greenfield, were recovered at lunchtime today.

Graham West (29), of Staley Drive, Stalybridge (father of three children) was found under tons of snow and ice. And there was no hope of finding alive the other man, Michael Roberts (27), of Cemetery Road, Dukinfield (father of five)—Both were officials of the Manchester Gritstone Climbing Club.

After the dangerous conditions had brought the rescue bid to a halt at midnight after nearly 12 hours of searching by police, the operation was resumed at dawn today.

Assisting the police were members of Royton ATC mountain rescue team, a RAF mountain rescue team and another from an army unit stationed at Preston.

The alarm was raised early on Sunday afternoon by two Greenfield youths, members of the same climbing party, and who had also been swept from the rock face by the avalanche.

'The Wilderness'

One of the survivors, 16-year-old Allan Wheeler, of North Avenue, Greenfield, told the Chronicle: "The other two were about 60ft ahead of us. Someone shouted "Avalanche!" and I was hit by several large pieces of ice and snow. The next thing I knew was being bowled over down the mountain side and ending up half-buried in snow."

Allan was pulled out by the other survivor, John Smith (19), of Warlow Road, Greenfield, who said: "I was behind the others when I heard a terrific crack. I shouted a warning and dived away. When I looked back I could see only Allan. The other two members of the party had disappeared."

At first the two survivors tried to find their missing companions. Then they made their way to Chew House, manned by Ashton

suffering from exposure, shortly before the search was called off for the night.

They were joined by more police under the supervision of Superintendent K. Wilburn—who had fought his way over in a broad-wheel-based jeep from Huddersfield—and Saddleworth Inspector John Chaddock.

'Fantastic'

An ambulance from Oldham stood by at Greenfield Paper Mill—which is being used as a base camp for the rescue operation—and the ambulancemen joined in the search.

One of them, Mr. William McGriffen, described the scene at the 200ft. gully as "Fantastic. I have never seen anything like it."

Also helping in the search have been 15 members of the Gritstone Club—including 24-year-old Tom West, of Gladstone Terrace, Green-

A GROUP of rescuers gather in the time office at Greenfield Paper Mill. Second from the right is Norman West, brother of Graham, one of the victims.

On the right is Allan Wheeler, one of the two survivors.

this area, but we have never known weather like this."

These two men—both members of the Gritstone Club—and about a dozen of their club mates had also been climbing in the Chew Valley area on Sunday and had last seen the missing men about 11 a.m.

Three-mile walk

Early today search parties were out again with shovels, including members of Royton ATC mountain rescue team who had spent the night

Headline news in *The Oldham Evening Chronicle* on 21 January 1963 reporting the avalanche in Wilderness Gully. The group of rescuers being briefed is probably part of Royton MRT.

The Coroner recorded verdicts of death by misadventure, and it was presumed that the children had succumbed to the cold and weather during the first night of their absence from home when a light dusting of snow had fallen. The story of why they went onto the moors has never been resolved.

There was certainly no shortage of enthusiasm to find the children; hundreds of searchers were involved and their control centred on Glossop Police Station. However, with no radios, little transport and few maps, monitoring the search must have been a nightmare. The morality of encouraging scouts, cadets, and schoolchildren as young as thirteen to search for the bodies of other missing children was surely questionable, and increased the likelihood of further mishap. A modern-day forensic officer must shudder at the thought of a potential crime scene being located by a search party so young.

1963: WILDERNESS GULLY AVALANCHE. TWO DIE

It was about lunchtime on Sunday 20 January 1963 when a group of four young men, all members of the Manchester Gritstone Climbing Club, were enjoying the winter conditions in Wilderness Gully in the Chew Valley, Greenfield. Suddenly there was a loud crack and as one of the party shouted a warning of 'Avalanche', his three friends were swept from the face and disappeared under hundreds of tons of snow and ice.

John Smith, from Greenfield, desperately searched in the icy debris and found Allan Wheeler, also from Greenfield, clawing his own way out of the snow. The two were dazed but spent some time trying to find their two companions, who had simply disappeared under the snow. Finally they had to give up and went for assistance from Chew House, an Ashton and District Water Board property. Water Board employees joined in the search but their efforts were fruitless and the police were alerted. Local police officers went back up to the gully and tried again to find the two missing climbers. One officer, PC Parkin, got himself into trouble when he fell through the snow into a deep gully. He turned up several hours later suffering from exposure and the search was then called off for the night.

The search resumed the following day with members of Royton ATC Mountain Rescue Team and an RAF rescue team, joined by an army unit from Preston. Later that day the bodies of Graham West and Michael Roberts were recovered from the avalanche debris and taken down to Greenfield.

Modern avalanche victim statistics demonstrate that there is very little chance of surviving a total burial for much longer than an hour as asphyxiation and hypothermia take their toll. However, this was another example of where there was no organised team of experienced people available to give immediate assistance, and a would-be rescuer nearly became another victim simply because of the lack of equipment and skilled knowledge.

1964: THE FOUR INNS. THREE DIE

It was in 1957 that, for the first time, thirty young men set out in groups of three to cross fifty miles of the Peak District's most difficult terrain on a walk organised by the 51st Derby St Lukes (California) Rover Scout Crew. The original route of the walk started at the Flouch Inn but it was rerouted in 1959 and now starts at Holmfirth, near to the site of another former inn known as the Isle of Skye. The route continued to finish at another pub, the Cat and Fiddle near Buxton, passing two other pubs on the way, the Snake Inn and the Nag's Head at Edale. It is not surprising then that the walk was known as the Four Inns and was to become a national and annual event. Although the length of the walk was reduced in 1959 to avoid confrontation with some landowners, it still remained a gruelling test of determination, stamina, and hill-craft.

Much of the route is around the 2,000ft contour and includes about 4,500ft of ascent and descent. By 1964 the popularity of the event had spread and eighty teams of three were to take part, with another forty teams having been refused entry because of the lack of accommodation. The walk was well organised with each competitor being handed information sheets with detailed instructions, routes and map references. The competitive teams would leave the start point at two-minute intervals from 06.00 a.m. onwards. Checkpoints were established no more than five miles apart at which competitors could obtain food and drink, and two rescue teams were on standby throughout the day.

It was an early start for the team from 32nd Huddersfield Rover Scouts, with Gordon Withers and his team mates Eric Rothery and Michael Kendal setting out from the Isle of Skye at 6.18 a.m. on Saturday 14 March 1964. The weather forecast of 'showers with fine intervals' gave no real threat of danger, but this was to be very misleading as the day deteriorated into heavy rain backed by strong winds. At 7.52 a.m. another team, this one from Birmingham University, set off on the walk; John Butterfield, Michael Welby and Robin Kydd all soon realising that the weather was not going to be kind as the wind began to sap their strength.

Tom Tomlinson, head PPPB warden, George Garlick, deputy head warden, and Trevor Wright, a PPPB volunteer warden, plan the search of Alport Moor in 1964.

Police and rescuers survey the steep sides of Alport Valley, 1964.

A line of searchers sweeps towards to the top of Alport Valley, 1964.

Glossop Rover MRT had little time for rest that weekend and was out at daybreak to continue the search in 1964.

WALSHS
'LINZI'
'MADAME L' DRESSES

Sheffield Telegraph

No. 33,836 MONDAY, MARCH 16, 1964. Telephones: 78585 General; 26393 Personal Announcements and Want-Ads Price 3d.

J. T. DOBB & SON LTD.

They braved the blizzard on the Derbyshire moors — one of the search parties who tramped all day in search of the missing Rover Scouts.

PEAK BLIZZARD TRAGEDY

One Rover Scout dies, two others missing

By DAVID SHARPE and KEITH FARNSWORTH

A teenage Rover Scout died in a raging blizzard on the Derbyshire moors yesterday, and late last night—after a massive hunt for two other missing youngsters—weary rescue volunteers said there was little hope of finding them alive.

The three boys were among 250 competitors taking part in a tough endurance test over a 40-mile course when the bleak rainswept moors suddenly changed into a "white hell." The Scout who died was 19-year-old Gordon Stewart Withers, of Bradley Mills Road, Rowthorpe, Huddersfield.

The two missing Scouts are John Butterfield, of Northcote, Lowmand Avenue, Wells, Somerset, and 21-year-old Michael Welby, of The Avenue, Lowestoft. A massive all-out hunt for them was called off late yesterday afternoon because of worsening conditions.

Eric Rathery (left) and Michael Kendall, two 19-year-olds who made a desperate attempt to save Gordon Withers. Michael staggered three miles to bring help.

Monday morning headlines break the news of the tragedy.

THE END ON MOOR OF DEATH

[illegible]DOWN FROM THE BLEAK ALPORT MOOR · POLICE AND RESCUE PARTIES CARRY THE LAST VICTIM OF THE BLIZZARD WHICH CLAIMED THE LIVES OF THREE ROVER SCOUTS OUT ON AN ENDURANCE TEST.

It was Tuesday afternoon before some of the estimated 370 people helping with the search finally brought the body of Michael Welby down towards the Snake Road.

Members of Royton ATC MRT searching the snow-covered Alport Moor in appalling weather conditions, 1964.

The Huddersfield team arrived at the Crowden checkpoint at about 11.00 a.m. and then set off for the Snake Inn. This is one of the toughest parts of the route with a steep climb out of the Longdendale Valley and then a tiring plod through the peat bogs to reach the summit of Bleaklow, followed by the shallow descent to the Snake Pass. All three rover scouts were very tired and wet through, but it was Gordon Withers who was suffering the most; he had started to stumble and needed the assistance of the other two to make any progress. The group set a compass bearing for Doctor's Gate but the weather and terrain drove them into the head of the Alport Valley, which actually extended the route they would have to walk before meeting with the main A57 road. About 2.00 p.m. Withers collapsed and the others decided they would need help to get him down to safety. Eric Rothery stayed with his friend Gordon whilst Michael went down the valley for help, arriving at Alport Farm about 2.45 p.m. A telephone call was made to the Snake Inn checkpoint and the Glossop Rover Scout Rescue Team was informed.

The rescue team had already been busy transporting other scouts from Doctor's Gate to the checkpoint so they could be fed and warmed up. Ray Davies, who was leading the team, sent a small reconnaissance party up to Alport Farm, whilst he would follow up with the rest of the team and a stretcher a few minutes later.

The three-man reconnaissance team quickly came upon two other exhausted scouts in the Alport Valley, who were assisted back to Alport Farm. Michael Dean, a member of the rescue team, continued up the valley and came across a third scout, David Rhead, lying semi-conscious on the path. Dean did what he could for the scout and then marked his position for the others to find before carrying on in search of Withers. Shortly afterwards Ray Davies and the stretcher party came upon Rhead lying against a sheep pen; his evacuation started downhill and other members of the rescue team coming up the hill to help soon met the party. The carry-off of Rhead continued down to Alport Farm, whilst Ray Davies and another rescuer, Geoffrey Tickle, started back up the valley in search of Withers, Rothery and Michael Dean. David Rhead was eventually taken to the Snake Inn checkpoint and then onto Woods Hospital in Glossop where he was treated for exposure and detained.

Michael Dean eventually found Eric Rothery and Gordon Withers lying in an exposed position in the Alport Valley. Rothery was suffering from cramp but was able to walk and on the arrival of Dean he set off down the valley to meet the remainder of the rescue party. Rothery shortly came across Davies and Tickle of the Glossop Rover Mountain Rescue Team and was able to tell them exactly where his friend Gordon and rescuer Dean were. Soon after, other members of the team escorted Rothery to the Snake Inn checkpoint. Eric Rothery had little idea at that time that he would later be identifying Gordon's body to the police at Glossop hospital. Gordon Withers and Eric Rothery had been friends for years and they had been team mates in the Four Inns competition the previous year, completing the course without any mishap.

Davies and Tickle continued up the Alport Valley and about a mile from the farm they came across Michael Dean supporting Gordon Withers. Withers's condition had deteriorated but he was still able to walk with some assistance and the rescue party attempted to move him to the sheltered side of the valley to await the arrival of a stretcher party. It was whilst they were moving across the valley that Withers staggered and may have caused the whole party to slip 20 or 30ft down the bank. Davies, realising the danger, jumped to support the party but then fell down into the river. He was not able to take any further part in the rescue and had to attend the local casualty department of Glossop Hospital where he was detained.

Members of the Glossop team and also the Edale team, which had been notified of the situation by the Snake Inn checkpoint monitor, continued the evacuation of Withers. The weather remained appalling with strong winds and now sleet. The rescue party had to cross the river several times in waist-deep freezing water and it was past 7.00 p.m. before they all arrived at Alport Farm. Withers was taken in a private vehicle, first to the Snake Inn checkpoint and then down to Glossop Hospital where he, too, was detained.

It was about 5.00 p.m. when a group of rescuers going up in support of the stretcher party came across another competitor named Robin Kydd, from the Birmingham University group. Kydd was totally exhausted and wet through but was able to report that one of his two companions was injured and that his other friend was staying with him in the upper reaches of the Alport Valley. However, Kydd was already suffering from hypothermia and he was unable to give the precise location of his friends. Kydd was escorted down to the farm where he was treated and warmed up. By the time the Withers rescue party arrived at the farm Kydd had recovered sufficiently to be able to give a better description of where he had left his companions.

Bryan Simm of Glossop Rover Rescue Team had now effectively taken charge of the rescue since Ray Davies had been taken to hospital. Simm went to the checkpoint at the Snake Inn and asked for New Mills Rescue Team to be called out; he also asked for assistance from the Control Point at Chapel en le Frith. Simm then took Gordon Withers by vehicle down to Woods Hospital in Glossop, arriving about 8.30 p.m. On admission to the hospital no pulse could be detected by the receiving nurse and Dr Waddell was called. The medical staff, assisted by police officers, attempted resuscitation for three hours and even tried using additional equipment brought over from the fire station but, at 11.00 p.m., Dr Waddell declared that Gordon Withers had died.

After taking Withers to hospital Simm returned to the Snake Inn to be told that a 'strong contingent' was coming from Chapel en le Frith and so the New Mills Rescue Team had not been called. Simms was not satisfied and contacted the Buxton police himself, asking for the support of the New Mills Rescue Team and an ambulance, for when the two missing scouts were found.

The rescue party from Chapel arrived shortly after and was taken up to Alport Farm by Simm. The Chapel team started to search the valley in the company of the farmer's son, but by now it was pitch dark and the weather had not relented. A second small team from the White Hall

Open Country Pursuits Centre near Buxton arrived under the leadership of Tom Tomlinson and they too went up the valley. New Mills team, under the leadership of Bill Thompson, assembled at Glossop Police Station at 10.00 p.m. and went to the Snake Summit to start searching from Bleaklow towards the top of the Alport Valley.

It was 3.15 a.m. on Sunday when the Chapel team returned to Alport Farm having found no trace of either John Butterfield or Michael Welby. The weather had turned from rain to snow, hampering transport and covering anything lying on the ground and this, coupled with the darkness, caused the search to be halted. It was then that the Glossop police started to organise a major search of the moors that would last three days and involve hundreds of police and volunteers.

There were many different organisations taking part including several mountain rescue teams, both civilian and RAF. However, the communications of the day did not allow for effective control of such numbers and it is likely that some areas were searched more than once and others left untouched. RAF Stafford was first to take proper control under the leadership of Sergeant May. The team had been notified of the incident in the early hours of Sunday morning and had travelled through the night from an exercise to arrive at Glossop by 6.00 a.m. Control was established on the A57 Snake Road at Doctor's Gate and all searching personnel were supposed to report there for instructions. However, on the Sunday the weather continued to deteriorate and at 2.00 p.m. the decision was made not to send any more searching groups onto the hill because of the falling snow. Those already committed to the moors returned and were stood down at 4.15 p.m.

Monday morning saw the arrival of a team of twenty-two men from RAF Leeming which, when added to the strength of the RAF Stafford team and an RAF ATC team from Royton, meant there was a good number of experienced and disciplined rescuers on the search. More importantly, they had portable radios to help control the search lines. An RAF search and rescue helicopter also arrived to assist. Search Control was moved to an RAF wireless truck in the lower part of Alport Valley and again all personnel were asked to report there for instructions. At 3.50 p.m. the first report of a body having been found was transmitted to the police and the find was confirmed at 4.40 p.m. when members of the Peak Park Planning Board Warden team, under the leadership of Tom Tomlinson and George Garlick, recovered the body of John Butterfield from the stream bed in the Alport Valley.

The search for Michael Welby resumed on Tuesday morning with an estimated 370 people sweeping across the Bleaklow moors. At 11.00 a.m. police officer Alan Jackson found Michael covered by snow in an area known as North Grain and the search was called off.

High Peak Coroner Mr Henry Hartley held a joint inquest into the three deaths on 8 April at Glossop. A long list of witnesses recalled their sad memories of the weekend and opinions were voiced on the inadequacy of the clothing worn by the scouts. The jury returned a final verdict on all three scouts of death by misadventure. The coroner noted the voluntary nature of the event and found that adequate information and warning about the route and equipment that should be carried had been given to all competitors. He found no evidence of neglect on the part of the organisers of the walk and concluded that every possible effort had been made by the search parties to find the scouts in appalling weather conditions.

The Scout Movement, under County Commissioner Clive Bemrose, set up its own inquiry into the events of the 1964 Four Inns Walk. Sir Jack Longland, president of the British Mountaineering Council, and a respected leading figure in the outdoor world, chaired the inquiry. The inquiry committee comprised thirteen people, ten from the scouting world and John Foster, PPPB Planning Officer, Tom Tomlinson, PPPB Head Warden and Kim Meldrum, principal of the White Hall Open Country Pursuits Centre at Buxton. Every aspect of the walking competition was reviewed and several recommendations were suggested to improve the organisation and management of the event. Nevertheless, the basic decision was that the walk should continue as an annual event but that much of the competitive nature should be removed to discourage participants from discarding the extra, and probably heavy, clothing that they should carry.

A final report was issued in August that year which emphasised the need to ensure that the competitors were better clothed and better equipped. The potential for exposure (mountain hypothermia) should be made clear to all competitors and they should be better informed as to its signs, symptoms and treatment.

The Committee of Enquiry also commented that the rescue organisation should be able to respond quickly enough to save life and be able to draw rapidly on sufficient organised and trained resources to meet the needs of a major incident. However, it was already known that changes were being proposed in the mountain rescue world, and a series of discussion meetings had already been held that would form the foundations of the modern service.

It should be noted here that the Four Inns Walk had been organised for the previous seven years and has since carried on as an annual event without any major incident. The event was well organised for its time but several factors were to conspire to turn the 1964 walk into a triple tragedy. With the benefit of hindsight we can look back critically, but we must also remember that many things taken for granted today were still unavailable forty years ago. The weather forecast was inaccurate but even today's highly sophisticated forecasting methods do not always get it right and a detailed forecast certainly was not so easily available.

The weather was bad and got even worse as the search was initiated, but it was the clothing worn by all the casualties that really let them down. The lightweight and breathable materials of today had not been developed and most outdoor enthusiasts looked to the ex-army and navy shops for their equipment. If a garment was waterproof in 1964 then you can assume it was also very heavy and created so much condensation on the inside that it was hard to tell if it was waterproof or not. Jeans and cotton materials are now known to be potential killers, for when they get wet they lose all the little heat-retaining properties they have. Wet cotton becomes heavy and cold and allows the wind to pass straight through it; wool, too, loses its heat-retaining properties when wet and becomes very heavy. Two of the deceased were wearing trousers made from cotton and all had cotton anoraks. None of the lads had any waterproof garments whatsoever, no gloves and only one had a hat.

Mountain hypothermia is now well understood and, although it is still a very real threat to anyone out in the mountains in the winter months, its onset and treatment form the foundation of every basic hill-craft course now available to novice hill-goers. The designers of modern mountain clothing understand the life-threatening effects of wind chill, and lightweight, comfortable materials have been developed that retain their warmth whilst wet. Waterproof shell garments repel heavy rain but still allow condensation to pass to the outside, keeping the wearer warm and dry on the inside. The only downside is the attached price tag. Food and nutrition are also better understood within the outdoor world. Lightweight, high-energy food and drinks are available in supermarkets and, whilst in the opinion of the authors, nothing replaces the satisfied feeling gained from eating a cheese 'door-stopper'; we all know that it is the high-protein, high-fibre and glucose foods that the body needs to survive and protect itself from the elements.

Mapping, too, has moved on in leaps and bounds in fifty years. 1:25000 scale maps are now readily available for the whole country and often in a waterproof format. Liquid-filled compasses settle quickly and accurately and a current position can be continuously monitored using global satellite technology. Such is the advancement of navigation technology that some of the old methods are being forgotten in favour of keyboard skills and minicomputer screens. Fine until the battery runs out!

A small and discreetly placed plaque serves as a memorial to the three lives lost on Bleaklow.

A brief inscription scratched onto a rock served as a temporary memorial stone.

Communications in 1964 relied almost totally on landline telephones, whilst today a mobile-phone signal reaches all but the remotest parts of the national park. At the time of the Four Inns tragedy the call box at the Snake Inn and the AA Box near Snake Summit were pretty poor substitutes; not even all the local farms would have had their own telephone line. Only a small percentage of police vehicles would have had a radio fitted and reception in upland areas was always very poor. On the hill only the RAF teams would have had portable radio sets and these were heavy and bulky. Communication was often by the use of thunder-flashes or coloured smoke flares, which were effective only in good visibility and in line of sight. Now the modern mountain rescuer is more likely to set out without his butty box than his personal mobile-phone and radio. Bluetoothed wireless gizmo pods now keep people in touch anywhere in the world as long as there is a network signal and, of course, the battery lasts!

The 1964 Four Inns tragedy was a terrible waste of three young lives which must have devastated their families. However, the event is already acknowledged as the turning point in the story of Peak District outdoor pursuits from which the modern mountain rescue service was born. The names of Gordon Withers, John Butterfield and Michael Welby will not be forgotten, as they will always feature in the history of the organisation dedicated to preventing any such loss happening again.

Ode to the Four Inns

Come all you scouts that roam the tops and hear what I do say.
Come all you Manchester rambling lads that roam the Pennine Way.
Come all you brave mountain climbing lads that scale the gritstone crags
and I'll tell of a snowstorm on Kinder Scout that killed three rover lads.

For the moorlands are a wicked place from Peak to Bleaklow Hill
and the Moss and clough will fool you and the weather change its will.
It's a lovely land in the springtime but beware if you should climb
for the moorland mists will catch you unprepared at any time.

On the fifteenth day of March the scouts set out with fun and talk
on a fifty mile endurance hike they call the Four Inns Walk.
They were only dressed for a ramble when a blizzard crossed their skies
Michael Welby, John Butterfield and Gordon Withers, all lost their lives.

For it's many a mile from Glossop to the stream at Doctor's Gate
and the snow was falling thickly as the scouts they came up late.
They were not dressed for a blizzard and the snow it numbed their bones,
it would be the last time that these poor lads would ever see their homes.

Origins unknown.

FOUR

1964: BIRTH OF AN ORGANISATION

The Peak Park Planning Board appears to have been the first organisation to react to the problems highlighted by the Four Inns tragedy of March 1964, when John Foster, the planning officer, called a meeting of his full-time wardens to discuss the situation. It was realised that the contact details for search teams were held at Derbyshire Police Headquarters at Matlock and any request for these teams to be called out would be routed through there. In practice it was thought that the contact details were possibly out of date and in any case local police stations such as Glossop were initiating their own call-outs. The meeting resolved to suggest to the police that any future calls for search teams should be directed to the Edale Rescue Post, which in turn would call other teams if necessary.

John Foster was also one of those instrumental in arranging a meeting at White Hall Open Country Pursuits Centre, Buxton, on 4 July 1964. The meeting started at 2.00 p.m. and was chaired by Alfred Pigott representing the MRC, and co-chaired, owing to the late arrival of Pigott, by Jack Longland, representing the British Mountaineering Council and Derbyshire Education Committee. A guest at the meeting was Colonel Jack 'Rusty' Westmorland who had founded Keswick MRT and who was able to report on the system that was currently operating in the Lake District. In total fifty-one people attended the meeting representing twenty-six different interested organisations.

The meeting opened with a report from the police stating that since the tragic loss of the scouts in March a further eight incidents had occurred where rescue teams had been required. J. Needham, representing the Derbyshire Cave Rescue Organisation, stated that after the death of Neil Moss in 1959 they had adopted a system whereby a list of seven controllers had been lodged with the police specifying who should be contacted in the event of an incident. The controller decided which teams to call and the leader of each team contacted called out its members. Colonel Westmorland outlined a similar system operating in the Lake District using eight team leaders as controllers. He also added that the Lake District's panel was considering buying 'walkie-talkie' sets but the drawback was that they weighed 4lb each.

The meeting decided that the best way forward was to set up a working party to examine the future organisation of mountain search and rescue operations in the Peak District National Park. Ten people were selected to form the group, which was to be chaired by Kim Meldrum, Principal of White Hall Open Country Pursuits Centre, and included Noel Kirkman as medical adviser and Ray Davies from Glossop Rover Scouts.

Alfred Pigott stated that the MRC would be able to designate Glossop Police Station as a Rescue Post and would also supply morphia and a full complement of rescue equipment for it. The PPPB agreed to the purchase of 2,500 copies of the British Mountaineering Council's circular on mountain exposure, costing 1*d* each, to be freely distributed to all wardens and other interested people.

Following that exploratory gathering, the initial meeting of the working party was hosted by the White Hall Open Country Pursuits Centre on 22 August 1964 and was to be the birth of the Derbyshire Mountain Rescue Organisation. The organisations represented were the Peak Park Planning Board, White Hall Open Country Pursuits Centre, Derbyshire Police Force,

Above: Emblem of the Peak District Mountain Rescue Organisation.

Left: Noel Kirkman OBE FRCS tends to his casualty.

Derbyshire Cave Rescue Organisation, Glossop Rover Mountain Rescue Team, RAF Stafford Mountain Rescue Team, New Mills Mountain Rescue Team, Glossop Moorland Rescue Team and the Mountain Rescue Committee. The originally proposed group of ten had swelled to thirteen and included Fred Heardman, PPPB Voluntary Warden, and George Garlick, PPPB Deputy Head Warden at Edale.

The police representatives pointed out that much of the national park was the responsibility of police forces other than Derbyshire and that representatives of those forces should be invited to future meetings.

The meeting agreed the proposal for 'an efficient call-out system to aid casualties in the hills'. The proposed call-out system involved each team being allocated to its own local Divisional Police Office and the police calling the team directly in the event of a small incident. However, the Police Information Room, then at Matlock, would call on a 'Search Panel' to handle longer or more complicated incidents. The panel members were nominated at the meeting and it was agreed that one or more would be called to control any searches that the police deemed necessary. The first search panel consisted of Kim Meldrum (White Hall Centre), Dr Peter Andrew, Fred Heardman, one warden from the PPPB, one representative each from Glossop Rover MRT and Glossop Moorland RT, William Thompson of New Mills MRT and one representative of Derbyshire Cave Rescue Organisation.

An open meeting of interested parties was called to examine the report of the working party and was held at Buxton Police Station on 19 September 1964. This time the team leaders of all the established rescue teams were invited. Teams which sent representatives were 51st Derby Scouts, the Gritstone Club, the Rucksack Club, the Ramblers' Association Mountain Rescue Club, Sheffield University Students Union, New Mills MRT, Glossop Moorland RT, Glossop Rover Scout MRT, Stocksbridge MRT, RAF Stafford MRT, South Ribble Fell Search and Rescue Team, Goyt MRT, Northern Command Territorial Army Medical Unit, 29th Sheffield Scouts, Edale MRT and Barnsley Mountaineering Club. The Birmingham Cave and Crag Club was unable to send a representative but had stated by letter that it was available for rescue work and had provided a call-out list. It was also noted that a team was being formed in Buxton.

Dr Peter Andrew OBE (centre), a life-long worker for the cause of mountain rescue, calls for calm in a busy incident control room during a multi-team search exercise held in the Derwent Valley. Ray Davies (Glossop MRT and Incident Controller) looks on from the right whilst John Mayer (Buxton MRT, now Call-out Officer) gently pollutes the atmosphere with his pipe. Mrs Joyce Poulter (Edale MRT) can be seen holding a clipboard.

Glossop Rover Scout MRT, *c.*1959.

The meeting agreed to change the name of the group from Derbyshire Mountain Rescue Organisation to the Peak District Mountain Rescue Organisation, thus better reflecting the proposed area of operations. Representatives of Cheshire, Staffordshire and West Riding police forces were also at the meeting and agreed that when an incident occurred in their own county they would inform the Derbyshire police and request the assistance of the Search Panel. It was also agreed that all incidents occurring anywhere in the national park, no matter how trivial, should be reported to the Derbyshire police for record purposes.

Three primary objectives for the organisation were agreed:

To assist the police authorities in attempting mountain search and rescue work in the Peak District National Park.

To co-operate with all kindred bodies and be prepared to assist with mountain rescue work in other areas.

To assist in non-mountain rescue work so far as this is within the capability of the organisation or its members and provided that the request comes from a police authority.

The organisation also stated that it did not undertake to rescue any person in distress, above or below ground, but would make best endeavours to render any assistance within its powers having due regard to the hazards to life involved.

Just a week later, at 2.30 p.m. on 26 September 1964, the inaugural meeting of the Peak District Mountain Rescue Organisation began. The full Search Panel was in attendance, being Kim Meldrum (White Hall Centre), Tom Tomlinson (PPPB Head Warden), George Garlick (PPPB Deputy Head Warden), Bill Thompson (New Mills MRT), P. Olive (Glossop Moorland RT), Dr Peter Andrew (New Mills MRT), Fred Heardman (Edale MRT), Ray Davies (Glossop Rover Scouts MRT), Inspector Sanderson (Derbyshire police) and J. Needham (Derbyshire Cave Rescue Organisation).

Some basic qualifications for member teams were discussed and agreed. All teams should have at least twenty-four members and be capable of presenting at least twelve on any call-out. Team members should be experienced mountaineers with training in first aid and particularly the treatment of exposure. Each team should have at least one car with a roof rack so as to be able to transport equipment. It was agreed that the average time to call out a team should not be longer than one and a half to two hours, all team members should be familiar with all the moors of the Peak District, and that team members should not speak to the press about any incident.

The panel also agreed that panel members running an incident should stay at the Incident Control and therefore those members who were currently also team leaders should stand down from that position and their teams would have to elect new leaders.

At 7.00 p.m. the same day the various rescue team leaders held a meeting to approve the setting up of the Search Panel. The meeting was chaired by Kim Meldrum and represented were Derby Scouts, the Mountain Club (Staffs), the Ramblers Association, the Gritstone Club, the Rucksack Club, Sheffield Students Union, New Mills MRT, Glossop Moorland RT, Stocksbridge MRT, RAF Stafford MRT, Glossop Rover Scouts MRT, South Ribble MRT, Goyt MRT, Northern Command, 29th Sheffield Scouts, Edale Rescue MRT and Barnsley Mountaineering Club.

The concept and membership of the Search Panel were accepted and agreed and each team made a statement as to its own strengths and capabilities. There was much discussion on the call-out procedures to be adopted but a decision was reached after recommendations from Inspector Sanderson. All calls for mountain rescue assistance in the national park, from anywhere in Derbyshire and the surrounding counties, would be passed to Derbyshire Police Headquarters. From there the first available member of the panel would decide on the next course of action depending on the circumstances of the incident.

Kim Meldrum closed the meeting by reminding teams that much practice would be necessary and that a major exercise was already being planned.

The building blocks of the current organisation were now in place but it would take a number of years before the present day structure would fully emerge. The Peak District Mountain Rescue Organisation in 1964 basically consisted of a Search Panel of ten people and a number of affiliated rescue teams on which the Search Panel could call if necessary. Beyond the four aims of the organisation there was no constitution or other set of governing rules. The panel took on the administrative duties and was to meet regularly but only occasionally did the full contingent of panel and team representatives come together.

There had been very few developments in technology at that point and any specialist equipment that was available was very expensive. Communications were still the biggest problem. Although the telephone network was becoming more widespread not every team member would have been connected. Calling members out was therefore time-consuming and often still relied on a pyramid system where one member had to contact two others on the list below him who would contact another two on the list below them. Communication on the hill was even more difficult. Only the RAF teams had any portable radio equipment and that was usually very heavy and mounted on specially constructed backpack frames. Once a team was committed to the hill it was very difficult to call it back other than to use smoke flares, thunder-flashes or, in one recorded case, ringing the chapel bell. There was also a shortage of money as the teams forming were often starting completely from scratch and very often had only youths as members. Some teams did not even own their own stretcher but relied heavily on the equipment kept at the MRC Rescue Posts.

In retrospect it is obvious that there were too many small and disorganised teams, but this was a new and emerging organisation. Anyone could start a rescue team, as there were no legal standards to meet, no registration and no regulation. It was during this era that the image of mountain rescue was tarnished by a few small groups of young men, purporting to be a rescue team, occasionally waiting with a Land Rover at sites such as Stanage Edge for a climbing accident to occur. It is charitable to imagine that these groups saw themselves as providing a service but in the eyes of others they were egotistic, incompetent idiots. Needless to say this practice upset many true outdoor enthusiasts and particularly the rock-climbing fraternity. It reflected badly on the whole of mountain rescue and particularly frustrated those who were working hard in an effort to build a genuine and responsible organisation. The friction and suspicion created between climbers and rescue teams has taken a long time to heal. It is perhaps only in recent years that climbers, having seen modern rescue team members administering advanced levels of first aid to seriously injured rock athletes, have regained trust and confidence in the organisation.

Other teams and individuals were trying hard to improve the service but each team varied tremendously in both its strength and ability. Many teams were, or had been, based on scout troops or cadet units and their membership was very young and inexperienced. Others were developments of climbing clubs and often drew their membership from towns well outside the Peak District.

ROYTON ATC MRT

One such team that deserves a special mention was a unit of the Air Training Corps. The Air Training Corps (ATC) was formed in 1941 as a development of the Air Defence Cadet Corps, which had been founded three years earlier to encourage boys to take an interest in aircraft

Royton ATC MRT proudly display their equipment *c*.1955.

with the ultimate aim of recruiting young men into the RAF. Following the war the ATC carried on its work, encouraging boys to join the forces and to promote good citizenship. At Royton, in north-east Manchester, the 1855 ATC Squadron had its headquarters in an old cotton warehouse where 130 or more boys regularly swapped their school uniforms to become young airmen. Training covered various topics allied to aircraft and flying and there was also a very active motorcycle unit teaching maintenance and encouraging road safety. The corps also taught camp-craft and hill-craft and promoted outdoor exercise and fitness.

During the war years several aircraft crashes had occurred in the Peak District and so the corps decided to start its own mountain rescue team. Royton ATC MRT soon formed links with the RAF Harpur Hill MRT at Buxton and was later officially recognised by the RAF as a sub-unit.

During the 1950s–60s the Royton ATC was under the command of Squadron Leader Bob Kenworthy, who had joined the unit as a Warrant Officer in 1941 and who had always enthusiastically encouraged the activities of the rescue team. The team was comprised of young lads, full of enthusiasm but with little experience. They had equipment typical of the time and of the forces – service-issue type boots, large mess tents and a folding canvas ambulance stretcher. However, the unit did have radios, which would have been the envy of any civilian team of the same era. Their equipment was transported in a trailer towed behind a Land Rover and the team members would often travel to the incident by motorbike.

Despite their youth they presented an organised and disciplined body, one of few to which the police could turn in the event of an incident on the moors. Situated north-east of Manchester, the team was well placed to travel into the mid-Pennines and as far as the Lake District.

Their call-outs were proudly recorded on boards, much like you might see in a lifeboat station, and started with a call in 1953 to search for a missing boy. The boards display their attendance at several incidents in the Peak District, including three air-crashes, the 1962 Chew Valley avalanche and the 1964 Four Inns tragedy. The team dropped out of the Peak District Mountain Rescue Organisation in the early 1970s because the young age of its members conflicted with insurance requirements. However, the team remained active until 1980 when the call-out board's last record reads, 'Missing hiker, Pennines'.

Royton ATC MRT on the road with their fleet of motorcycles, *c.*1955.

Noel Kirkman OBE FRCS (far right), MRC chairman and MRC president, escorts a casualty party down the Chew Valley.

THE CHRONICLE, April 4, 1964.

Saddleworth and Mossley

'ALL CLEAR' AFTER CREVICE MYSTERY

FEARS that a pot-holer might be trapped down a narrow crevice on top of Duckstones—a boulder-strewn hill on the Saddleworth moors—were dispelled after police and a mountain rescue team had climbed 1,700 feet up Chew Valley at Greenfield on Tuesday.

The alarm was raised on Monday night by two Manchester fellwalkers after they had seen a rope hanging down into the yard-wide crevice.

A small contingent of police and members of Royton A.T.C.'s mountain rescue team who made a preliminary investigation by torch-light could see no sign of life and a full-scale search was put off until today.

The 20-ft. rope was not of a type normally used by climbers or pot-holers and it had been there for some days.

Checks on missing-person files proved negative and inquiries were made at local farms in case the rope had been used in a sheep-rescue operation, but these also failed to throw any light on the mystery.

After a thorough search had been made this morning, Inspector John Chaddock, who led the Saddleworth police party, said they were satisfied that no one was down the crevice.

No marks

He said it was possible to get down to a depth of 12 feet, and then the gap narrowed to about 1ft. 6in., making it almost impossible for anyone to get any further.

There were no marks to indicate that anyone had fallen and moss in the crevice was not disturbed.

Inspector Chaddock said a probable explanation was that youngsters had been playing there and left the rope, intending to return later.

Another theory was that the rope had been deliberately "planted," as it was of a type being used on the near-by £2 million Dovestones Reservoir scheme.

Squadron Leader R. Kenworthy headed the Royton ATC party. First to go down the crevice were Barry Thompson (19), of Lilac Grove, and Tony Brook (19), of Parkfield, both Chadderton, followed by Squadron Leader Kenworthy and Inspector Chaddock.

While the Royton ATC team worked at the scene the Oldham-based East Lancashire Mountain Rescue Team stood by.

Inspector John Chaddock, of Saddleworth, is helped out of the crevice after calling off the search.

ATC helped in search for fell-walker

AFTER an emergency police call early on Saturday morning, 11 members of Royton ATC mountain rescue team made a 90-mile dash to the Lake District to help in the search for a missing fell-walker.

He was 49-year-old Reginald Harper, of The Boulevard, St. Annes, who had set off on Wednesday to walk over the fells. **His car was found later that day and a search started when bad weather set in, and Mr. Harper had not returned home.**

Then on Saturday morning, Royton ATC were called in by Lancashire County polce and asked to help in the search. Eleven men made the journey by Land Rover and car, and were searching in Loughrigg Fell, when Mr. Harper's body was found in the near-by Borrowdale Fell at about 3 p.m. on Saturday.

Above: Newspaper cuttings from 1964 record the exploits of the Royton Team.

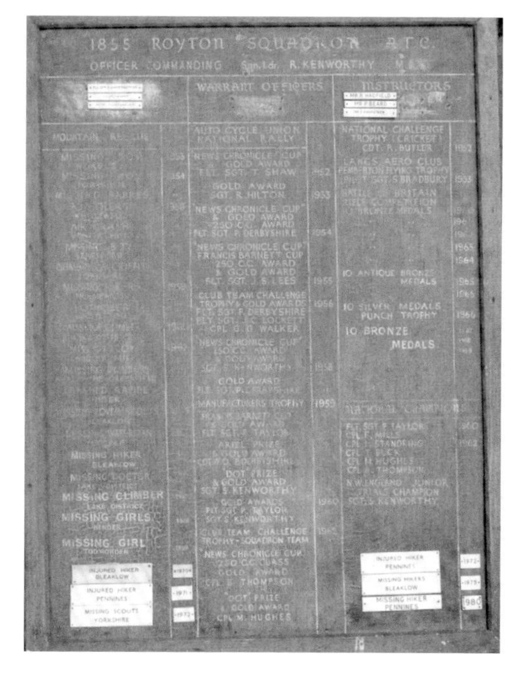

Right: The incident board from Royton ATC Headquarters depicting each call-out from 1953 to the last record, 'Missing Hiker, Pennines 1980'.

FIVE

1971: A CRUNCH EXERCISE

On the night of Saturday 23 January 1971 Sergeant John Brewer of RAF Stafford and Dr D. Bunting launched 'Exercise Crunch' at the request of the PDMRO. The exercise scenario was that of an air crash on Bleaklow, with mock living casualties provided by RAF Stafford MRT and RAF St Athan MRT, and many dead ones being simulated by plastic bags. It did not go well!

A debrief of the exercise was held on the following Saturday at Glossop Police Station chaired by Dr Peter Andrew. Twelve teams with over 240 rescuers had taken part and so, unsurprisingly, communications were blamed for some of the problems, but other more serious concerns were voiced. Control of the incident seems to have been somewhat chaotic and uncoordinated but actions on the hill were worse. One observer commented that he saw, 'A considerable number of team members who were ill equipped and poorly trained. Some were fourteen years old and in plastic macs and shoes!' The twelve teams could muster only nine stretchers and three of these belonged to Glossop MRT. Radio procedure was criticised as was first-aid training and equipment, for instance sleeping bags were being used in place of proper casualty bags.

In his summing up of the debrief meeting Dr Andrew is quoted in the minutes as saying 'The panel needs to think carefully about its co-ordination and future control but team leaders too must think about the membership of their teams. We will learn from our mistakes on a practice and there is obviously a need for better training and practical exercises between teams.'

MARCH 1971: RADICAL PROPOSALS

Other meetings quickly followed and proposals for a radical shake-up of the organisation were made. Fundamental to the proposed changes was the creation of an Administrative Committee to watch over the broader aspects of rescue and to be separate from the operational Controllers' Panel, formerly Search Panel, which would manage all incidents. The individuals making up the proposed Controllers' Panel would, in the main, be the professionals involved, including National Park Wardens, police, RAF Stafford, and Doctors Andrew and Bunting.

The proposed Administrative Committee would include all the controllers plus representatives from the Derbyshire Cave Rescue Organisation and the landowners, a chief inspector from Derbyshire Police Control Room, the principal of White Hall Open Country Pursuits Centre and the leaders of each of four named rescue teams.

The four teams, to be known as Initial Operation Teams, were those that had already proved their training standards, equipment levels and all-round ability to be acceptable. They were Glossop MRT, RAF Stafford MRT, Edale MRT and Buxton MRT. Other teams wishing to be included were invited to arrange an exercise to demonstrate their suitability.

The requirements for 'Initial Operation Teams' status, laid down in the proposal by the PDMRO, were:

Young faces of the Sett Valley Team on exercise in the William Clough area, *c.*1965.

Police officers assist with a casualty evacuation. Note the polished shoes, just what every well-dressed rescuer used to wear.

The carry-off continues on an MRC Post stretcher.

Team members learning the basics of rope management on the crags. This is a simple technique called abseiling, allowing the individual to lower himself down a rock face without any special gadgets. In more modern times a device would be used to lock off in the event of the rescuer letting go of the rope. Current health and safety practices mean that he would probably also have a safety rope attached.

Members of Huddersfield Rover Scout Team dealing with a casualty on a MacInnes stretcher. Only one team member wears a helmet in a situation where all members would be required to wear head protection today.

A minimum of thirty members.
All members to be competent and equipped to traverse the Peak District moors in any weather, day or night, and be able to navigate in bad conditions.
A minimum of twenty-five percent of members must hold an Adult First Aid Certificate.
All members must know the symptoms and treatment of Exposure as published in BMC Circular 380, revised March 1968.
All members to be able to handle a mountain stretcher (which the team should have) on Peak District terrain. This would include using ropes to descend steep slopes, including in winter conditions, but would not require every member to do crag rescues. However, at least half the team should be able to participate in a crag rescue.
The teams must hold regular training exercises and invite members of the committee to assess the teams' abilities in the various techniques above.

1 The Four Inns Walk in later years. Here one of the groups is counted as it passes through a checkpoint at one of the highest points on the course.

2 Derby MRT in the early 1970s with Vernon Poulter (kneeling centre), John Tomlinson (standing centre) and Steve Hilditch looking over his left shoulder.

3 Buxton MRT training for the recovery of an injured casualty from a rockface. A first-aider and one barrow boy helper are already tending to the patient, and a folded Alphin stretcher is on its way down the crag with the second barrow boy. Once at the same level as the casualty the stretcher would be unfolded and attached to each barrow boy's rope before the casualty is loaded. The barrow boys then control the lower to ground level using Alp descenders.

4 The same crag rescue scenario but this time demonstrated by visiting members of Ogwyn MRT using their prototype stretcher.

5 Woolly hats, check shirts and knee breeches were the order of the day in the 1960s and a real mountaineer would also have had a beard and a drooping pipe.

6 Team members boarding a Sea King helicopter. The maximum carrying capacity depends on the weight of fuel still remaining but the aircraft can carry up to four crew and nineteen passengers. The modern search and rescue helicopter is nearly twice as fast and can operate for nearly three times longer than the first Whirlwind helicopters.

7 The Peak District is served by helicopters from RAF Leconfield which is just over thirty minutes' flying time away, depending on wind direction.

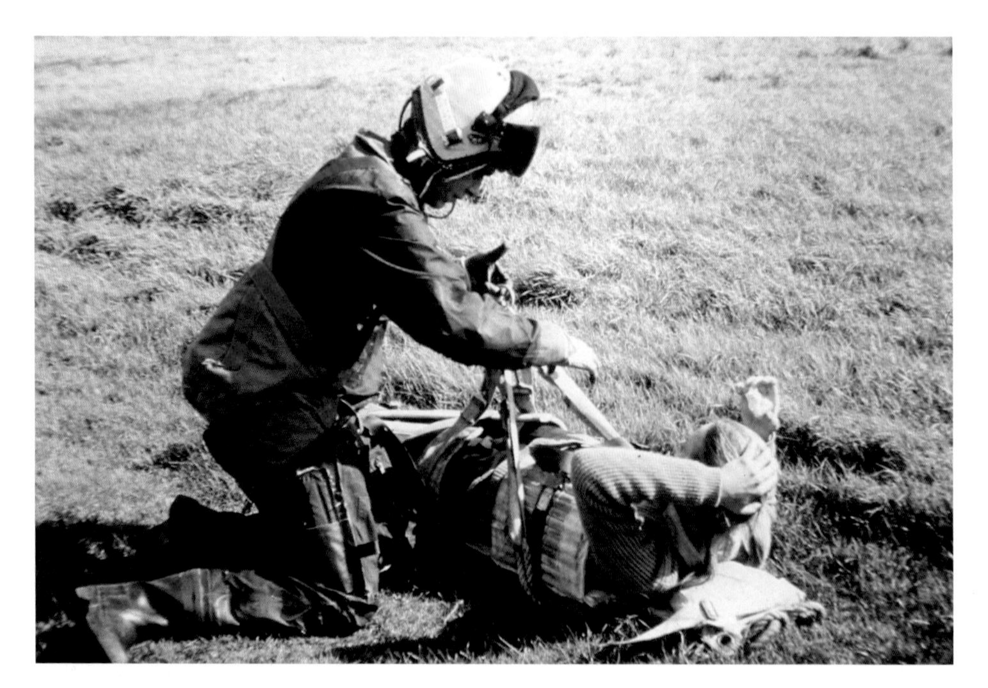

8 The winchman from an RAF Sea King prepares a mock casualty for a lift in a Neil Robertson stretcher. The aircraft carry both a Neil Robertson stretcher and a basket stretcher. For mountain rescue purposes the aircraft will also lift any of the normal stretchers used by teams but access through the door can be a problem.

9 The weather closes in on Kinder Scout as an injured walker is assisted to The County Air Ambulance by a Peak District National Park ranger and Air Ambulance paramedic.

10 An Air Ambulance helicopter takes a patient off the Buxton Mountain Rescue Team at the Roaches in Staffordshire. The small aircraft of the Air Ambulance fleet are ideally suited to landing in confined and sometimes uneven spaces. Internally they are very cramped with space for the three-man crew and the casualty only. They do not have any winch mechanism and therefore the casualty must always be carried to the aircraft. All the Air Ambulance fleet are operated by charities and their availability can depend on funding.

11 Air Ambulance paramedics and a mountain rescue doctor treat an injured climber at Stanage Edge whilst the remainder of the Edale/Buxton snatch squad prepare to transfer the casualty to the aircraft waiting on the top of the crag.

12 Lessons have been learned and teams are now equipped with buoyancy aids and life lines and regularly train in water safety techniques.

13 Buxton team members fix ropes on the upper tier of The Roaches in Staffordshire in readiness for the lowering of an injured climber.

14 Surprisingly no injuries were sustained and the remains of the aircraft were eventually and rather ironically airlifted to the Snake Summit and onto a waiting low loader lorry. See page 37.

15 A sweaty, smelly and potentially dangerous job now left to the experts.

16 The winch-man kneels nonchalantly at the door of an RAF Sea King Helicopter as it approaches to land on the moor, delivering a Buxton MRT section.

17 The Controllers' Panel receive their 'Chief Constable's Commendation' certificates presented by David Coleman, Chief Constable of Derbyshire Constabulary, at police headquarters on 12 November 2001.

18 The authors' first meeting in Wildboarclough, Macclesfield Forest, in 1977, where they decide to write a book in thirty years' time!

It was proposed that Initial Operation Teams would be called first in the event of a missing person and would be backed up by the other teams if the situation escalated. Teams that were not allocated initial operation status were asked to provide stand-by cover at either Edale or Crowden at weekends and on Bank Holidays to respond to any known-location accident. This proposal reflected the problems of communications and the delays inherent in calling out teams.

The full PDMRO committee, including the controllers and representatives of eleven teams, met at Fieldhead Information Centre on 1 April 1971 to discuss the proposals. Such radical changes caused some heated discussion but, with just a few amendments, the reality and practicality of the proposals were accepted by the majority and the proposals were carried. The necessary variations to the organisation's Constitution were discussed and a decision was also made to seek formal recognition as a charity. Ray Davies, leader of Glossop Rover Scout MRT at the time of the Four Inns incident, was also elected to the Controllers' Panel.

This landmark meeting heralded the changes that were to create the PDMRO as it is today. The people and teams involved have since changed but the basic structure has remained the same. Whilst the aims of the organisation have not altered, the role of mountain rescue has matured and the expectations of the service have become more demanding. Over the last thirty-five years the outdoors has become increasingly popular for all sorts of recreational activities. The nature of incidents today reflects those changes with a far greater proportion of known-location accidents to missing persons being reported. Developments in transport and communications have been steady and the rescue service has adopted as much of the new technology as it can afford.

The issue of radio communication was one of the first problems to be addressed by the new look PDMRO. Following a major fundraising campaign the PDMRO could afford to buy six of the new 'transistorised' Pye Bantam radios together with one base station set. The sets were kept at the Edale Information Centre and, in return for their licensing and servicing, the national park staff could use them when they were not required for rescue purposes. If they were needed for a rescue they were collected in and taken by road to the Incident Control Point.

Just a few years later Derbyshire police agreed to provide Peak District mountain rescue teams with a complete radio network including licensing and servicing. Each team received a number of hand-held portable radios and two base station sets to replace the miscellany of radio equipment that they had acquired over the years. Since then the sets themselves have been renewed a number of times and the frequencies used have changed but the Derbyshire constabulary still provides the hardware. This has been a very significant contribution to the rescue service over the years and has saved the PDMRO teams many thousands of pounds.

As time moved on nearly every team member would have a home telephone and the time taken to call out a team started to fall. However, there was another problem. Teams were struggling to turn out sufficient people to daytime incidents as many members could not be released from work, yet others, who worked near to the accident hotspots, were available but not being contacted because they were a member of another team. Ken Drabble, PPPB Head Warden at Edale and a PDMRO Controller, proposed a new system for calling out team members during the working day.

The system was to be known as the 'snatch squad' and revolved around pre-prepared lists of people who worked closest to the regular rendezvous points, regardless of which team they belonged to. In the event of an incident being reported during the working day the appropriate snatch squad would be called. The techniques used by the various teams were by now so similar that mixing up members of different teams had little effect on the efficiency of the evacuation. However, team training was developed to cover management of snatch squad incidents on the hill so that everyone knew who was in charge. A new title of 'Incident Site Officer' emerged and it was agreed that the first senior member to arrive at the scene would adopt the role and don a yellow jacket for identification purposes.

Woodhead MRT dealing with an injured casualty lying on a ledge of a gritstone outcrop. It appears as if the rescuers have climbed up to the casualty where normal tactics in the Peak District would be to lower the rescuers from the top.

In the early 1970s the fire service was called to Mam Tor near Castleton where two young boys tried to climb the shale face, soon realising it was not as easy as it looked. The climb starts at an easy angle and then sharpens in to a near vertical final pitch. The face of Mam Tor is not rock but shale and as the boys moved on to the steeper parts they found their footholds crumbling away. Buxton and Edale teams are regularly called to similar incidents today. The rescue can be dangerous for climber and rescuer alike as the face is so unstable and large boulders are easily dislodged. The teams have often thanked the Ordnance Survey for placing a triangulation pillar at the top of Mam Tor as it provides the only suitable belay (anchor) point.

One of the boys safely reaches the top and is greeted by firemen and Pete Freeman, then PPPB information officer. PDMRO rescue teams would be called to this incident if it were to happen today; however, Derbyshire Fire and Rescue Service does have a rope rescue unit stationed at Matlock. The unit is regularly first on scene at many of the classic limestone crags which tower above Matlock Bath.

Police officers confer with rescue team members on the A57 Snake Pass Road during a search operation. An RAF Team Land Rover is parked just behind the police car.

Derbyshire police moved its headquarters from Matlock to a new building opened by the Queen at Ripley in July 1977. The new control room covered the whole of the county and yet not a single computer is in sight!

The Derbyshire Constabulary emblem.

Modern times with Buxton and Edale team vehicles at a 'snatch squad' rendezvous. Both teams use the equipment from whichever vehicle arrives first, keeping the second vehicle free to attend any other incident which may be subsequently reported.

Edale/Buxton snatch squad ready to transfer a casualty from the rescue stretcher onto the ambulance stretcher. Most snatch squad calls are often close to a road and usually of a short duration. Team members rarely waste time changing into full hill gear before they set off to such incidents as time can be crucial when dealing with a seriously injured casualty.

Hilary Briars, PDMRO Snatch Squad Officer, juggles two telephones at her home in Chinley during a call-out, *c.*1994.

The PPPB Information Centre and Ranger Briefing Centre at Fieldhead, Edale, in the early 1990s. This building opened in June 1966 to replace a tin building that had served as the Information Centre since 1959. The MRC Rescue Post equipment was kept in a small building at the rear but the stretcher hung inside the centre as part of a display. For many years the Information Centre was the first point of contact during daytime hours for the police wishing to call out mountain rescue. The building was demolished in 2006 to make way for a new 'Moorlands Centre'.

In practice the snatch squad system was administered by Mrs Hilary Briars from her home in Chinley, and it was she who maintained the lists and badgered members to keep their contact details up to date. During the working day all calls for mountain rescue received by the police would be directed to the PPPB Information Centre at Fieldhead, Edale, which could contact any of the wardens/controllers by radio for advice. In the event of a call-out requiring a snatch squad for any area of the Peak District the controller would inform Hilary of the incident details, which list to use and the rendezvous. Hilary, ably assisted by her neighbour, Joan Cooper, would then start telephoning each individual at work. As they gained experience and got to know many of the switchboard operators at the other end, the time it took to make the calls got shorter and shorter and it became a very efficient operation.

The snatch squad system was always somewhat controversial but it was very successful from the casualty's point of view as members were getting to the incident site quickly. However, it also meant that those members who worked in the national park and were regularly available during the daytime were being called to nearly every incident and so became very busy. Consequently, those living further away were not being used as often and some also objected to the other teams working on their patch.

The introduction of a radio-pager calling system in September 1995 meant that just one telephone call could alert all members of a team at once. Teams started to withdraw from the system in favour of using their own call-out officers and the principle of the snatch squad became redundant, with one notable exception. Edale and Buxton teams together covered possibly the busiest areas of the national park where straightforward and often short-duration incidents frequently occurred. These teams both recognised the advantages of a joint response during the working day and agreed to continue with it. The two team system continues to operate very successfully to this day and always guarantees to turn out sufficient members even in busy holiday periods.

SIX

TEAMS: THEN THERE WERE SEVEN!

The formation of the Peak District Mountain Rescue Organisation in 1964 provided the police with a central point of contact for civilian rescue teams and negated the need to appeal for a wider response from the general public. The numerous *ad hoc* groups of rescuers that appeared spontaneously at the Four Inns incident were never to be used again, but there was still a large number of organisations purporting to be able to form a rescue team. It is difficult to count the actual number of organisations that supposedly were affiliated with the PDMRO in 1964, as each set of records and minutes uncovered seems to vary. However, documents found from around this era mention the following:

Barnsley Mountaineering Club
Barugh MRT
Birmingham Crag and Cave Club
Birmingham University Climbing Club MRT
Buxton MRT
Buxton Scouts MRT
Cave and Crag Club MRT (Staffs)
Derby 51st Rover Scout MRT
Derbyshire Pennine Club
Dewsbury Adventure Club
East Lancashire Moorland Rescue Team (Oldham)
Edale MRT
Glossop Rover Scout MRT
Glossop Moorland MRT
Goyt MRT
Gritstone Club
Holme Valley MRT
Huddersfield Rover Scouts MRT
The Mountain Club MRT (Staffs)
New Mills MRT
Northern Command Rescue (Territorial Army Medical Unit)
Oldham Rover Scout MRT
Oread MRT
RAF Stafford MRT (formally RAF Harpur Hill)
Royton ATC MRT
Sett Valley MRT
Sheffield 29th Rover Scout MRT
Sheffield Union of Students
South Ribble Fell Search & Rescue Team
Stocksbridge Rover Scout MRT
Ramblers Association MRT
Woodseats' Police Search and Rescue Team

This photograph is thought to be of the RAF Harpur Hill team in action, *c.*1955.

How active these teams ever were is difficult to establish as very few records have been uncovered that relate to more than just a few of the organisations. The minutes of the first ever team leaders' meeting held in September 1964 record statements by some of the organisations relating to their strength and ability which vary widely. Derbyshire Pennine Club declared it had nine members whilst Sheffield Union of Students stated it could contact 4,000 students within minutes!

A natural levelling of the number of teams occurred between 1964 and 1975. It is believed that many of the organisations never actually managed to form an active team and, of those that did, many folded well before the shake-up in 1971. The creation of Initial Operation Teams in 1971 set standards which some teams were never going to be able to meet. The minimum age requirement was one factor that affected the teams that depended on scouts or cadets for their membership. Some neighbouring teams amalgamated whilst others, which realistically were never likely to be called to an incident because of their geographical position, folded. However, other teams were gaining in strength and respectability and would eventually emerge as part of today's PDMRO. Of the original list of thirty-one known organisations professing to be rescue teams only five still exist in one form or another, and two new ones have been created by amalgamation. Modern communications and transport enable teams to respond quickly to any part of the area and, if necessary, they can quickly deploy to the opposite side of the Peak District in support of another team coping with a complicated rescue or multiple incidents. There is no longer a need for a team in every valley and fewer but larger well-organised teams can make more efficient use of charitable funds. The process of evolution will surely continue into the future as the costs of running a mountain rescue team continue to escalate.

The last team to drop out of the system was from RAF Stafford, formally RAF Harpur Hill. RAF Stafford MRT, which had a long and distinguished history of service to the area starting from the war days, closed in 2005 and transferred to RAF Valley on Anglesey. This left just seven rescue teams in the Peak District, all civilian and all members of the PDMRO.

BUXTON MRT

White Hall Open Country Pursuits Centre stands at 1,300ft above sea level on Long Hill at Buxton, overlooking the head of the Goyt Valley. Originally a manor house, it was taken over

Above left: The first emblem of Buxton Mountain Rescue Team.

Above right: 'The Pig', Buxton's ambulance, built in 1953 and its Ford Transit equipment van. These were the pride and joy of the team in 1978.

by Derbyshire Education Committee in the late 1940s and, with the vision of Jack Longland, Director of Education, became one of the earliest outdoor pursuit establishments in the Peak District. Peter Mosedale was its first warden and, borrowing ideas from the scouts and the outward-bound centres, he started an education programme using volunteer instructors. In 1955 Geoff Sutton took over as warden and by now the White Hall Centre had a reputation for having a good staff of mountaineers especially skilled in climbing and caving. It was Sutton who first offered the services of the White Hall staff to help in mountain rescue when the Voluntary Warden team was being established in 1956. Wilson Hey, whose name is synonymous with the supply of morphine to rescue posts, lived at Fernilee, very near to White Hall, and was a regular visitor to the centre. It was through his efforts that White Hall became designated as an MRC Rescue Post and was supplied with a stretcher. White Hall staff were regularly involved with rescues and searches and the centre was one of the first units to be called to the 1959 Neil Moss caving tragedy in Peak Cavern at Castleton.

Eric Langmuir became principal of the White Hall Centre in 1959 and it was while he worked there that he, Jack Longland and John Jackson of Plas y Brenin developed specialist training courses which would eventually result in the formation of the Mountain Leadership Training Board in 1964. Kim Meldrum followed Langmuir as principal of White Hall in 1963 and he thus became a central figure in the negotiations that eventually resulted in the formation of the PDMRO. Meldrum chaired many of the early formative meetings held at the centre and was eventually nominated as a member of the first Controllers' Panel. The world famous climber Joe Brown was employed at the White Hall Centre during this era and his name is recorded on the minutes of several early meetings. The White Hall Centre also hosted the first ever conference organised by the Mountain Rescue Committee in October 1962 to which Rescue Post Supervisors from all over the country were invited.

It was during Eric Langmuir's time as principal that Howard Hodgkinson joined the staff of instructors. It was in conversation with Howard that Eric Langmuir suggested that a more

Above left: Buxton team's most famous casualty. In 1977 Coronation Street's Ken Barlow (Bill Roach) was carried by team members to a waiting RAF helicopter for the twice-weekly ITV soap. This incident must also hold the team's record for the longest carry-off as it took three episodes to complete.

Above right: Bill Roach presents then Team Leader, Ted Burton, with a Hare traction leg splint bought for the team by Buxton Junior Chamber of Commerce.

formal rescue team be formed in Buxton using the expertise of some of the staff. Hodgkinson contacted members of Buxton Caving Club, notably Dave Allsop, and members of the Buxton Walking Club. The authors have not been able to uncover any paperwork relating directly to the formation of Buxton Mountain Rescue Team but are fortunate to be able to rely on the testament of Howard Hodgkinson, its first team leader.

The team was up and running by mid-1963 and in the early days would use the equipment from the White Hall Rescue Post. The first team meetings were held in the Eagle public house on Buxton Market Place and later at the Roseleigh Hotel on Broad Walk. The team began to acquire additional equipment and in 1972, for £130, it purchased an ex-military Austin ambulance built in 1953. Fondly known as 'The Pig' because of its lack of power steering and crash gearbox, the vehicle was kept at Buxton Police Station. John Mayer, who joined the team in 1965 and still serves today as call-out officer, remembers, 'We would get the call to assemble outside the Eagle pub but the man who kept the key to the equipment store lived in Matlock and we would have to wait for him to arrive before we could set off. Often by the time we got to the incident it was all over.' However, despite such snags, the Buxton team was one of the first to obtain Initial Operation Team status in 1971 and was allocated the call sign 'Zulu'

In February 1974 team leadership passed to Ted Burton who was to guide them into a new era and pushed for improved training and resources. In 1976 the team became the only rescue team in the country to be accepted as a Division of St John Ambulance. Early relationships with St John were a little difficult as the team refused to wear the uniform or conform to some of the other regular duties expected of a Division. However, under the guidance of team member Gordon Booth, a keen St John first-aid trainer, the standard of casualty care in the team quickly improved. The relationship with St John went from strength to strength over the years and is now particularly relevant in this age of certificated training courses.

In 1977 the team sought a building in which to store its equipment and was offered a disused garage rent-free with a storeroom at a quarry in Dove Holes. Some renovation work was carried out and the team eagerly moved in. The Pig and a second elderly van were scrapped and the team updated itself with a second-hand Leyland Sherpa van.

In 1989 the quarry owners gave notice to the team that the base site was required for redevelopment and this led to an intensive period of fundraising and publicity to find another site for the headquarters. Negotiations with Dove Holes Community Association resulted in the granting of a free ninety-nine-year lease on a piece of land on which the team was encouraged to build a new base. The building was duly erected and to the team's great pride was opened with great ceremony by HRH Diana, The Princess of Wales, in June 1990.

Ted Burton was to lead the team for fifteen years until 1989 when he stood down and Roger Bennett was elected to be team leader for the following five years. Ted Burton was soon accepted onto the PDMRO's Controllers Panel and also served as team president for a short period. In the 1999 New Year's Honours List Ted was made a Member of the British Empire for services to mountain rescue in the Peak District.

In 1999 the team reviewed its operational status and decided to embark on a long and expensive modernisation programme for its equipment and facilities. Project 2000 was launched and the team set about raising the money to replace two vehicles, provide a mobile control trailer, renew the team members' operational clothing and, most importantly, build a new and larger base. Nearly £165,000 was raised in an amazingly short time and building started in 2002. The whole project, which had been planned to take at least five years, was completed in March 2003 when the purpose designed building was opened by HRH Prince Andrew, The Duke of York. In that same year the team received the 'Queen's Award for Volunteers in the Community', and in 2007 Derbyshire County Council recognised the team with an 'Excellence in the Community' award.

The team's base occupies a position by the A6 in Dove Holes just north of Buxton, permitting easy access towards both the White Peak and the Dark Peak areas even in winter road conditions.

The Dove Holes base which served Buxton MRT between 1977 and 1990. A small and cramped building by today's standards, it nonetheless provided a garage with a classroom above. Mod cons included a tap and electricity although the resident mice often chewed the cable and caused a blackout, and being centred in a working quarry all the equipment had to be dusted off before it could be used. However, the most important factor was that it came rent free. The quarry owners generously tolerated the team for nearly thirteen years before redevelopment of a brick-making plant caused its demolition.

Left: Roger Bennett, then Team Leader, escorts HRH Diana, The Princess of Wales, on the day of the official opening of Buxton Mountain Rescue Team's new base on land owned by Dove Holes Community Association in June 1990.

Above: Ian Hurst, BMRT chairman, invites HRH Prince Andrew, The Duke of York, to unveil a plaque to mark the opening of the team's new operational headquarters in March 2003. This building created garage space for three vehicles with an incident control room above. The older building was converted into a classroom providing a spacious training area and completing a long project to update the team's facilities.

DERBY MRT

Derby Mountain Rescue Team sprang into being as a direct result of the Four Inns incident in March 1964. The 51st Derby Rover Crew was the scout unit that had organised the event since its inception in 1957 and its members were understandably shocked by the tragic events on that walk. They felt a moral obligation to do something positive and it was not long before the idea of a Derby Scout Mountain Rescue Team became a reality. Representatives from Derby Scouts attended the inaugural meetings of the PDMRO and the Derby team was one of the first to become affiliated. The team was allocated the call-sign 'Romeo' and would support other teams in searches of the Peak District. Dave Cowley was the Rover Scout Leader at the time and became the first leader of the new rescue team. Rowley Wood from 4th Derby Scouts became the first chairman and the task of building a team from scratch began. The unit had little rescue equipment but it did have the experience of years of scouting to draw on.

In the event of an incident the team used the pyramid method of calling out its members. This was a difficult and time-consuming system at best but, before mobile phones and radio pagers, there was little option and most teams used a similar method. Transport was a major problem because, with such a young membership, few members had vehicles of their own. The team would meet at an agreed initial rendezvous point, usually the rear of the Friary Hotel in Friar Gate, Derby, where those with transport could assist the less fortunate and share costs.

As with most teams the very early records, if there ever were any, have been lost but it is known that Derby MRT's first recorded call-out was on 30 September 1968 when, along with

Left: Emblem of the Derby Mountain Rescue Team.

Middle: Dr Griff Pugh (3rd from left) and his group of doctors and assistants. Members of the 51st Derby Rover Scouts acted as 'guinea pigs' for Dr Pugh's investigations into hypothermia.

Bottom: Derby MRT members training with members of the PPPB Ranger Service. Then team leader, Steve Hilditch (kneeling right) demonstrates a casualty being loaded onto a Bell stretcher. Also pictured, left to right, are: Peter Jackson, Les Nuttall, Tony Hood, Paul Barlow and Mick Blood.

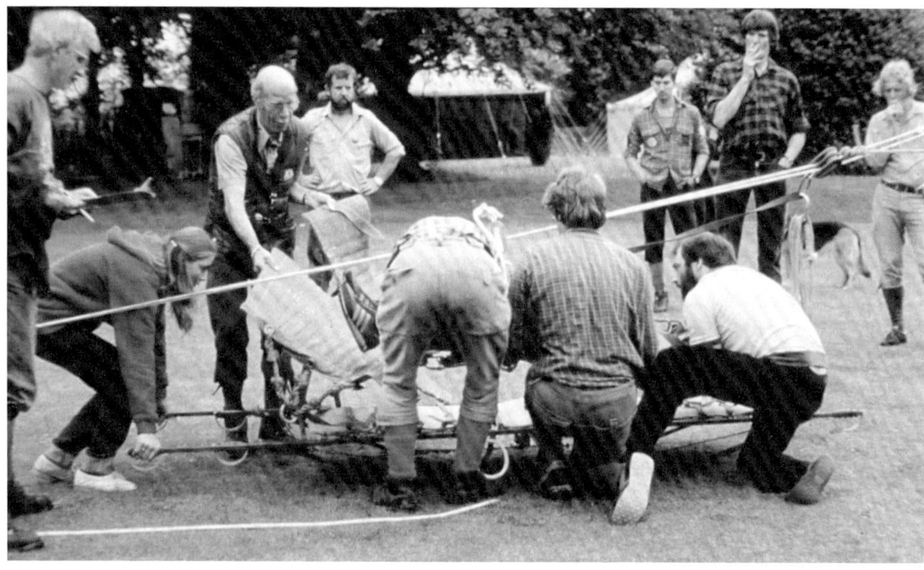

Derby Mountain Rescue Team's early transport.

Edale MRT in around 1968, comprising paid and voluntary PPPB wardens. Standing, left to right: Jack Lavender, Gordon Miller, Margaret Bailey, Jack Lees, Brian Jones, -?-, -?-, George Garlick (team leader), Frank Eyre, -?-, -?-, Dave Forshaw, Eddie Wilshaw, -?-, Ian Hurst and Ian Milne. Front row: -?-, -?-, Jean Lomas, Les Nuttall, Malc Padley and Eric Plumbtree.

other teams, it went onto Kinder Scout above Hayfield to search for two missing girls. The team continued to respond to search calls but was rarely used for known-location incidents, due mainly to the distance its members had to travel.

However, the team was never shy to respond to calls from even further away and in April 1973 travelled to Ogwyn Cottage in North Wales to assist in a major search for four boys taking part in a Duke of Edinburgh Award expedition. Eighteen members made the journey and joined a local force of 420 already searching. The boys were located and rescued by helicopter working just ahead of where the Derby Team was being deployed. The event is celebrated in the Derby team's history as being the first time Peak District teams (Stocksbridge MRT also attended) had worked outside the normal area of operations.

The PDMRO Controllers are reputed to have objected to the teams having gone out of the area without first consulting the panel; however, any dispute must have been quickly resolved for in November 1973 another major search was to be organised in North Wales and this time Derby was one of several PDMRO teams that went to assist. This search – for Peter Diamond – was to last three days, covering a staggering 200 square miles and utilising 1,100 searchers drawn from rescue teams, outdoor pursuit groups and mountaineering centres. The search was unfortunately fruitless and Peter's body was not found until five months later, well camouflaged and hidden in a cave.

In 1975 the team underwent assessment by its peers in the PDMRO and successfully achieved Initial Operation Team status. The team had started to move away from its scouting origins and controls and the leadership of Vernon Poulter, since 1972, had been fundamental in improving training and the commitment expected from its members. Sadly, a degenerative and eventually fatal illness forced Vernon's retirement. Dick Griffiths served briefly as team leader in 1977 but was unable to continue and Vernon resumed as leader until 1981. Vernon's illness was such that Steve Hilditch actively held the role of team leader Designate from 1979 until his election to the full post in 1981. Steve has continued as leader to the present day.

The team continued to progress, much in line with other teams, as technology and funds allowed and the expectations of the police and public rose. Two members, Mike Crome and John Tomlinson, were involved in the search for the missing scouts in 1964 and have continued their service unbroken to this day. Robin Knott was also involved in the 1964 search and has continued his membership with just a short break. These three – along with others – have strived to make the team the successful and greatly-respected unit it is now. All three have also been involved with the organisation of the subsequent Four Inns Walks.

EDALE MRT

The story of Edale Mountain Rescue Team starts with the creation of the Peak District National Park in 1951, the negotiation of open access to the hills and consequently the forming of the warden service in 1954.

The PPPB, having invited the public to come and use the Peak District hills, shouldered some responsibility for the accidents and mishaps occurring to its visitors. The Access and Footpaths Sub-committee was administered by the then Planning Officer, John Foster. By 1955 he was receiving regular reports of incidents from his Head Warden, Tom Tomlinson, and from Fred Heardman who was licensee of the Nag's Head in Edale, which also served as an information point. Foster supported requests from Tomlinson and Heardman for rescue equipment to be kept at Edale and negotiated with the Mountain Rescue Committee for Edale to become recognised as a rescue post. The PPPB sponsored the cost of a Thomas stretcher and a first-aid kit to be kept at the Nag's Head under the watchful eye of Heardman.

Emblem of the Edale Mountain Rescue Team. The team received the 'Queen's Award for Volunteers in the Community' in 2007.

Mike Hammond (standing, far right) became Edale Team Leader in 1971. He had previously been a member of Glencoe MRT and brought a depth of knowledge with him when he came to the Peak District as a full-time PPPB warden. Mike is seen here instructing a group of volunteer wardens in stretcher-handling techniques using a Thomas stretcher probably borrowed from the Edale MRC Post.

Full-time PPPB rangers, Gordon Miller and Ian Hurst, take the full weight of the stretcher as they pass a narrow part of the path on the evacuation route from Grindsbrook to Edale. Grindsbrook leads up onto Kinder Scout and, until recently, was the start of the Pennine Way and has been the scene of many similar stretcher evacuations. This later photograph shows the Bell stretcher from Edale MRC Post which replaced the old Thomas stretcher.

Dr David Dalrymple-Smith, a long and faithful servant of mountain rescue in the Peak District, leads Edale MRT back from a night carry-off.

Edale members practicing on the overhanging limestone cliffs of Plumb Buttress in Chee Dale. The overhang makes a normal approach from the top very difficult and here the rescuer is being forced to swing into mid-air. Plumb Buttress is a classic rock climb and teams no longer practice there for fear of damaging the rock-face. However, at about 10.00 p.m. on a November evening in 1990, Buxton team was called to the crag to rescue two climbers who had been stuck on the face for over six hours. Their faint calls for help were heard by a resident of the lonely Blackwell Mill cottages as she was putting the cat out for the night. Without that slight stroke of luck the climbers would have been on the rock-face all night and may well have succumbed to the weather.

Heardman and Tomlinson's local knowledge allowed them to find sufficient local people to assist in the event of an accident, but a search for a missing person called for more volunteers. Heardman was asked to contact the clubs that had helped form the Voluntary Warden Service and seek additional people to help in the event of a search. After several meetings and practice exercises the Voluntary Warden Search and Rescue Organisation was formed in 1956. In 1959, Fieldhead Information Centre at Edale opened to the public and the rescue post equipment was transferred across from Cooper's Café where it had been temporarily kept during construction work.

Tomlinson, Heardman and the Voluntary Warden team were kept active through to 1964 and the events of the Four Inns tragedy. The life and work of Fred Heardman, who died in 1973 aged seventy-seven, have been commemorated by the creation of a small patch of woodland known as Heardman's Piece on the slopes of The Nab behind his old home, the Nag's Head.

After the Four Inns incident the PPPB, with John Foster and others, was instrumental in arranging the meetings of interested bodies that would bring about the creation of the PDMRO.

With the PDMRO now established, a meeting of the Access and Paths sub-committee on 15 January 1965 officially recognised 'the establishment of a warden rescue service comprising thirty part-time patrol wardens which will operate from the rescue centre maintained by the Board at Fieldhead, Edale and whose activities will be supervised by the Board's Head Warden'. Edale MRT was born with George Garlick as its leader and Don Aldridge as deputy leader.

The team continued as part of the PPPB Warden (now Ranger) Service until October 1984 when a review of the PDMRO recommended that the Sheffield section of Woodhead team

Left: The strikingly tall figure of George Garlick, PPPB deputy head warden (later head warden) at Edale and first team leader of Edale MRT, using one of the new Pye Bantam radios.

Above: Emblem of the Glossop Mountain Rescue Team.

should join Edale. The team still works closely with the PPPB but it no longer requires its members to be wardens and it no longer receives any financial help from the park authority.

The team gained the support of the owners of Hope Valley Cement Works and moved its vehicles and equipment into a spare garage unit there. Space was always at a premium, and in 2007 Lafarge Aggregates generously agreed to increase the garage space and allow the team to renovate the existing building, which was specially opened in October 2007 by Mr John Bather, Lord Lieutenant of Derbyshire.

Covering many of the 'play areas' of the Peak District National Park, including the eastern climbing edges, the team is the busiest in the PDMRO and now deals with over 100 incidents per year.

GLOSSOP MRT

The modern Glossop MRT can trace its history back to the very day that it was decided to form a team. Glossop town occupies a crucial position in the Peak District, being at the Western end of the A57 Snake Pass and close to the A628 Woodhead Pass. Both these roads cut through some of the highest and wildest moorlands in the area and give unequalled access onto Kinder Scout, Bleaklow Moor and the steep-sided valleys of Crowden in Longdendale. The formation of a rescue team in Glossop was an obvious and natural progression as rambling became popular and access to the higher moors opened up, but it was not until the late 1950s that any formal unit was established.

The adventurous activities of the Rover Scouts were very appealing to the lads in the mill town and it is in the scouting movement that the team has its origins. A group of would-be Rover Scouts had their first meeting in Glossop on 19 November 1957 and a healthy and

Glossop team on the grim search for the bodies hidden by the Moors Murderers in October 1965. Ray Davies (fifth from the right) leads the team.

Glossop Rover Scout MRT searching the deep snow of Alport Valley on 16 March 1964 in the hunt for Michael Welby.

thriving Rover Unit was soon established. Two years on, at a meeting on Monday 20 April 1959, the Rovers decided to form a mountain rescue team. Inspector Guest from Glossop Police was invited to talk to the Rovers on 4 May and the Glossop Rover Mountain Rescue Team was born. The crew quickly established links with the National Park Voluntary Warden Search and Rescue Organisation and it was on 4 July 1959 at a training event in Edale that the team had its first recorded rescue; it was called to assist in the evacuation of a girl suffering from an ankle injury on Kinder Scout. The team started a logbook of events that provides a unique archive of the team's history and development from the very beginning.

As Rover Scouts the unit was already involved in the annual Four Inns Walk and some members would participate in the competition each year. It was natural then that the team should provide standby rescue cover for the walk each March. It was that fateful walk in 1964 that proved the bravery and determination of this band of young men who battled for hours in appalling conditions to help other scouts. The Glossop Rover Team, under the leadership of Ray Davies, played a significant part in the search for the three missing scouts and a police report following the incident commented:

> The behaviour of the Rover Scouts who took part in the initial searching for their companions is beyond praise. To be hampered by casualties under such shocking weather conditions required courage and stamina and constituted a tremendous feat of endurance. The leader of the Glossop Rover Crew Mountain Rescue Team, Raymond Davies, deserves special mention in this respect and was a wonderful example to his fellow searchers.

At about the same time another rescue team was being formed in Glossop that was to become known as Glossop Moorland Rescue Team. Following the foundation of the PDMRO the two teams decided to band together and became the Glossop Mountain Rescue Team that is still operating today. For many years the team was fortunate enough to have its base in a rent-free property at the rear of Glossop Police Station which had once been the dormitory of the old Glossop Fire Station. Renovation of the police station during 2005–06 forced the team to seek temporary alternative accommodation and, ironically, it became a guest at the new Glossop Fire Station. With renovations complete, the team was able to move back to Glossop Police Station in late 2007.

The team plays a crucial part in the present organisation, as the area it bears responsibility for is some of the most open and remote land in the Peak District. Whilst the area does not lend itself to some of the modern sports pursuits that give rise to so many of the rescue incidents in the park, the team has been the salvation of many a walker who, despite modern technical aids, has become lost on the bleak, windswept moors.

KINDER MRT

Kinder team has its base in Hayfield. nestling in the Sett Valley and under the shadow of Kinder Scout, the highest point in the Peak District. The small mill-working and farming community of Hayfield started to boom soon after the coming of the railway in the mid-nineteenth century. Whilst the railway was built for commercial use it also provided easy access for ramblers to ride out from the heart of Manchester and Stockport straight to the gateway of open country. The moors above Hayfield were in private ownership and jealously guarded by gamekeepers, but the railway meant that walkers were arriving in numbers and looking for ways onto the forbidden plateau of Kinder Scout. It is little surprise then that one of the most famous rallies in the fight for 'the right to roam' was to take place in 1932 in the Kinder Valley at Hayfield. The Mass Trespass, as it was to become known, was one of several such events organised around the Peak but this one became famous because five people were arrested. In July at Derby Assizes the five were given prison sentences ranging from two to six months to be served at Leicester Jail. In April 1982 a plaque commemorating the fiftieth anniversary of the event was unveiled on the rock face at Bowden Bridge car park.

With easy access from Hayfield onto Kinder the village was soon to become the centre of several searches and rescues but no rescue team existed until 1959. An MRC First-Aid Post was established at Reservoir House in 1950 but in Hayfield, unlike the Lake District or North Wales, there were no climbing huts or hostels from which to draw assistance; the visitors all went home by train, bus or car. The local police had to rely on the few local residents, shepherds, and water board workers who knew their way across Kinder to help out if an accident occurred or a person went missing. It was following such an incident that Police Sergeant Starkie was talking at the back of the New Mills Magistrates' Court to the then Probation Officer for the area, Bill Thompson. The two decided that they would form a mountain rescue team and Bill Thompson was to be its first team leader.

New Mills is about four miles up the line from Hayfield and, being a bigger town, had a greater population to draw on. Drawing members mainly from these two towns the team slowly grew in size, but did little training and relied on the MRC Rescue Post for its equipment. However, it did respond to several call-outs and was active in both the fatal Glossop incidents in 1962 and 1964.

Following the events of 1964 another scout team was formed, this time in Marple near Stockport. John Niell was the group leader at Marple Rover Scouts, joining forces with George Livingstone, group leader of High Lane Rover Scouts. Together they formed The Goyt MRT,

Sett Valley MRT operating near to Kinder Downfall, *c.*1965.

Positioned on the quarry wall at Bowden Bridge, Hayfield, this plaque commemorates the 1932 Mass Trespass.

Kinder MRT smartly turned out in new jackets outside its base at Hayfield.

drawing its members from the Rovers of both units but using the Marple Scout Hut as its base. The first recorded team leader was Bob Conway.

It was the 1971 shake-up of the PDMRO and the formation of Initial Operation Teams that prompted New Mills, by now known as Sett Valley MRT, and the Goyt team to amalgamate and form today's Kinder Mountain Rescue Team. The joint teams moved into the Sett Valley team's former base in a garage behind the George pub in Hayfield, but space soon proved to be a problem and they moved just next door into a larger part of the same building. The base was ideally situated at the head of the road leading directly to Kinder Scout, and the George pub has always provided a handy meeting venue.

The team has had some notable members who have worked hard, not just for the team, but also for mountain rescue in general. Dave Kirkpatrick, who became team leader in 1976 and served for thirteen years, went on to join the Controllers' Panel and be chairman of the PDMRO. Dr Peter Andrew was team doctor from the team's inception and worked tirelessly on behalf of mountain rescue. He served as chairman of the PDMRO and as vice chairman of the MRC between 1979 and 1985. He became chairman of the MRC between 1985 and 1995 when he was elected president of the MRC until his death in February 2000. In 1996 Dr Andrew was awarded the Order of the British Empire for his services to mountain rescue.

OLDHAM MRT

Oldham MRT is another team that can trace its origins back to the scout movement and the tragic incidents of the early 1960s. The Oldham Rover Scout Crew had members taking part in the 1964 Four Inns Walk and the unit later volunteered to help in the search for the three missing scouts. A few of the crew accompanied the police up onto Alport Moor and into Alport Dale and later that day witnessed one of the bodies being carried out to the Snake Road. It was perhaps the seriousness of this event and the memories of the two climbers having been killed in an avalanche in Wilderness Gully two years before that inspired the crew to establish the Oldham Rover Rescue Team.

The team affiliated with the newly formed PDMRO and made the Scout Headquarters at Glodwick Road, Oldham, its base until the early 1970s. Around this time the scout movement was starting to have trouble financing the operations of the team. The team decided to separate from the

Oldham MRT brings a casualty down the Chew Valley in winter conditions, *c.*1969.

Oldham Rover Team assembling ready for a training exercise, *c.*1964. From left to right: Geoff Dent; group of six unknowns; Hans Jungmayer (with the droopy sack); Barry Clayton (looking left); Ian Barrell; Dave Riley; Michael Ward (looking down); Andy Holt (back to camera). Others are unknown.

Oldham MRT members taking part in a crag rescue exercise on a gritstone outcrop.

Oldham team carry off a casualty on an Alphin stretcher. The lead rescuer holds aloft an intravenous fluid bottle which a doctor must have previously inserted into the patient to reduce any further effects of shock.

scout movement and register as an independent charity. George Dew generously offered the team the use of an old coach house near Tunstead at Greenfield to garage a vehicle. Shortly afterwards the team acquired a second vehicle, an Austin Champ, which was based at the Cross Keys pub at Uppermill, courtesy of Harold Nield. The early nomadic days continued when both the existing vehicles were replaced by a Land Rover and the team moved the garage to Stoneswood at Delph in a property owned by the local authority. Team meetings were held at the local police station but later space became available at Uppermill Police Station and the team moved on again. The cell served as the team's equipment store and an old courtroom was used for meetings until 1986 when Lees Brewery generously offered the use of an old barn adjacent to the Cross Keys. This offered sufficient space for garaging the vehicle, storing equipment and team meetings.

All was well for four years until one evening in September 1990 when a customer at the pub saw smoke rising from the barn. The fire brigade attended and managed to salvage the vehicle and the main structure of the building but everything inside was damaged by heat, smoke or water. Whilst the fire seemed like a disaster at the time the team was back and available for call-out within forty-eight hours, thanks to the generosity of the other local teams and emergency services. The brewery repaired the building whilst team members pulled together to clean, redecorate and re-equip the base. A public appeal for financial assistance was generously met and the building reopened better than ever and with suitable pomp and ceremony in late 1991.

Being at the north end of the Peak District region the team has been able to build strong links with mountain rescue teams in the Mid-Pennine area and has particularly good relations with the Greater Manchester police, fire and ambulance services. Members of the team have always been advocates of equipment and systems innovation and have, in association with outside companies, developed a stretcher and an aerial rope rescue system as an alternative to others commonly in use. The team runs an annual course in crag rescue, which is attended by members of teams from around the country and representatives from the paid emergency services. Oldham team, in the pursuance of improved communication, was the first team to introduce radio-pagers into the call-out system. A special and generous offer was made by Vodafone, from which all Peak District teams benefited, and was a major stride forward in the improved efficiency of the region.

The team is well situated at the west end of the A635 road to Holmfirth. This road gives access up and onto Saddleworth Moor and the north side of Black Hill. The local water authority has given permission for the team to use the private access road up to Chew Reservoir, which can offer fast access to the upper reaches of Great Crowden Brook and the Pennine Way to Black Hill.

The official opening of the new Oldham base at the Cross Keys at Upper Mill in 1988. Chairman of the Parish Council, Ted Lord, makes a speech to the gathered team members including, right to left: Dave Broadbent (then leader), Phil Kay (then landlord), Roy Cunningham, Dave Alport, David Henderson, Jim Duffy, Phil Beard, Geoff Smith, Dr Andy Taylor, -?-, -?-, Val Littlewood and Roger Kennedy.

Oldham team photograph in front of a Wessex helicopter.

Emblem of the Woodhead Mountain Rescue Team

Dave Crossland (far right), one of the founder members of Woodhead MRT, and other Huddersfield scouts on a navigation training day. The middle person is practising using a sighting compass which, when used correctly, can give pinpoint accuracy but which rapidly fell out of favour when liquid-filled Sylva compasses came on the market.

Above left: Huddersfield Scout Team carries a casualty off using a MacInnes stretcher.

Above right: Huddersfield Scout Team practising a vertical stretcher lower, *c.*1970.

Right: Huddersfield Scout MRT prepares its equipment for an exercise.

WOODHEAD MRT

Woodhead MRT is another team to trace its origins back to the Rover Scout movement and with a direct link to the Four Inns tragedy. Gordon Withers, who was one of the three scouts to perish that night in April 1964, was a member of 32nd Dalton, Huddersfield, Rovers. Following the incident, leaders in the Huddersfield area agreed to start a rescue team and join the newly forming PDMRO. The keen young Rovers owed much of their early training to Peter Blackley, an ex-RAF rescue team member, who was able to show them how to organise a sweep search and tie ropes to a stretcher.

Sheffield 29th Rover Scouts and Stocksbridge Rover Scouts had also had the same drive to form rescue teams in 1964. Logistically it made sense for these three teams to join forces with Barugh MRT from Barnsley and come under one administration. In 1975 the three Rover units and Barugh MRT joined together to become the Woodhead Mountain Rescue Team. The name

The result of the three scout teams merging into the modern Woodhead MRT.

Huddersfield Scout MRT with its ambulance in around 1971, probably the first team in the Peak District to have its own transport.

Woodhead accurately reflected the area of operation and was a name everyone had heard of, as the A628 Woodhead Pass was always one of the first roads in the area to be blocked by the winter snow. The former leader of the Huddersfield Rover Team, Barry Gregory, became the new team's first leader and later was to become a PDMRO controller.

In 1994 it was recognised in a review of operations by the PDMRO that the Woodhead and Edale teams' areas overlapped, and consequently the Sheffield section of Woodhead split off to become part of Edale MRT.

The team built strong relationships with South Yorkshire Ambulance Service and in the mid-1980s was given a Land Rover Ambulance with the promise of maintenance and fuel. By 1996 the team was considering its operational efficiency and concluded that it needed a base which was centrally located and which was large enough for training and equipment storage. Fortunately the team found the support of a local building firm from which it was able to lease an old farmhouse at a peppercorn rent. The building needed a lot of work to make it habitable but the renovation resulted in the ideal team base with more than adequate space and facilities including a helicopter landing pad.

SEVEN

SEARCH AND RESCUE DOG ASSOCIATION

The use of dogs to locate lost or trapped people is not a new science. In the seventeenth century pilgrims travelling to and from Rome through the Great St Bernard Pass in the Swiss Alps were sometimes grateful for the work of a local breed of dog called 'Sennenhunde', dispatched by the clerics of the Augustinian hospice to find weary travellers lost in snowstorms. The breed became known as the St Bernard, and St Bernard became the patron saint of mountaineers.

In later times the Red Cross used dogs to find injured servicemen on the battlefields of France during the First World War, and in the Second World War they were used to locate victims of the London Blitz.

The usefulness of search dogs in British mountain rescue was recognised by Hamish MacInnes who attended a training course for avalanche search dogs held by the Swiss Alpine Club at Engelbert in Switzerland in 1963. At the time Hamish was leader of the Glencoe Mountain Rescue Team in Scotland and whilst he knew the use of dogs for avalanche rescue in Britain would be limited he saw their potential for finding people missing in the mountains.

Hamish already had a German Shepherd bitch named Tiki and set about training her on the Scottish mountains. Hamish's wife Catherine was a doctor and she too was regularly involved with the work of the Glencoe team. She acquired a German Shepherd named Rangi that began training with Tiki and soon showed great aptitude for search and rescue. Rangi's success at finding buried avalanche victims became renowned and his exploits were the subject of a book of the same name written by Ernest Dudley in 1970.

Word about the successful work of the dogs quickly spread and in May 1965 Hamish held a meeting at his house that would lead to the formation of the Search and Rescue Dog Association. In December that year he held a training course in dog handling, which was attended by potential handlers from all over Britain. The Association went from strength to strength and the numbers of applicants meant that standards were kept very high. Successful dogs were graded into one of three qualifications. Grade A was for novice dogs that would be allowed to partake in daylight searches. Grade B was for the more experienced dog and, if the handler was a competent all-year-round mountaineer, the letter M was appended. Grade C was for the qualified dog and handler that had actually made a find during a call-out and had attended a course in Glencoe to prove the ability to locate in snow conditions.

By 1971 the Association recognised the logistical difficulties of operating a British-wide organisation and it was decided to split into three separate associations: England, Wales and Scotland. The English Association held its first formal training course in the Peak District in March 1972 when it elected to become an independent Registered Charity.

The pioneer of search dogs in the Peak District was Mike Hammond, who came to the area as a warden for the PPPB in 1969. Mike had been a mountain guide in Glencoe and a member of the rescue team. In 1965 Rangi and Tiki had a litter of seven pups; Mike acquired Tess and started training her for mountain searching. As a mountain guide Mike spent five or six days a week on the hills and Tess's potential was quickly realised when she got a Grade A pass in December 1966. On another training course in 1968 Tess was awarded a Grade B and was accredited as a fully trained search dog.

Above left: The logo of the National Search and Rescue Dog Association, established in 1971.

Above right: Emblem of SARDA England.

Above left: The logo of the volunteers dedicated to support and help with training search and rescue dogs. They attend events all over the country and in desperate weather conditions to provide a realistic scenario for the dogs and handlers.

Above right: John Combs, Edale MRT, with Search Dog Biscuit.

Mike Hammond, about to enter onto moorland to begin a search, looks with irony at the 'Dogs must be on a lead' sign.

Mike Hammond and Tess after a search at Crowden in 1971.

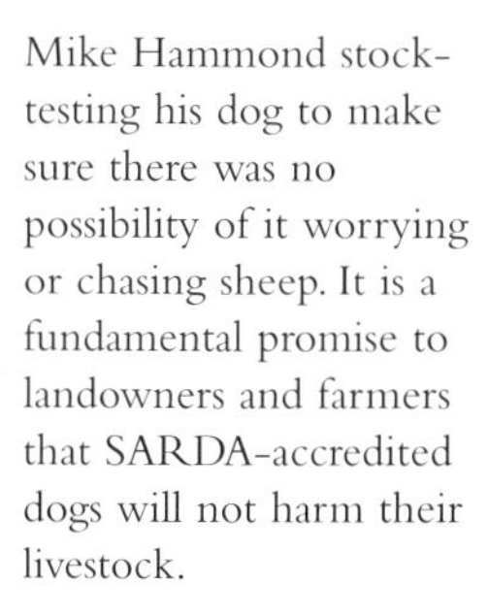

Mike Hammond stock-testing his dog to make sure there was no possibility of it worrying or chasing sheep. It is a fundamental promise to landowners and farmers that SARDA-accredited dogs will not harm their livestock.

Search Dog handlers, Dave Gregory and Mick Blood swap doggie stories during a break on a search at Fairholmes in the Derwent Valley.

Search Dog Tyke, with handler Ian Bunting, finds Dogsbody John during a training exercise

Mike Hammond became the first Area Organiser for search dogs in the Peak District in 1971, by which time there were five dogs either accredited or under training in the area. These included two bitches, Che and Kim, both born to Tess. Che was owned and trained by Mike and Avril Hammond and Kim was owned and trained by Jack Lees of Edale MRT.

The first recorded find by a Peak District dog was in 1971 when Tess located a group of teenagers missing all night in wet and windy conditions in the Crowden area. This find meant that Tess could be awarded the coveted Grade C status, and it was just the first of twenty accredited finds by Tess during an active service life that included over 100 search incidents.

Since then over thirty-six Peak District handlers with nearly fifty search dogs have passed through the rigorous training course set by the Search And Rescue Dog Association. There are

Search Dog Trig, with handler Malc Bowyer, outside the new Information Centre at Castleton.

Handler Bob James with Search Dog Sandy make a find in deep snow conditions.

many people who can thank the skill and dedication of these dog and handler partnerships for their salvation from the bleak Peakland moors.

The training and work of SARDA goes on and skills and techniques continue to develop. Whilst the early dogs were mainly German Shepherds, several other breeds have since proved to be as effective. The dedication required of the handlers exceeds all other aspects of mountain rescue, with time-consuming training an ongoing process that never stops until retirement. The British search dogs have never carried a barrel of brandy but the sight of one of these skilled dogs appearing round a peat hag on a dark and stormy night has a far better morale-boosting effect than any alcohol.

EIGHT

EQUIPMENT

PERSONAL EQUIPMENT

Fashion is the single biggest dictator in the choice of mountaineering equipment today! A thought-provoking statement and one with which some will argue, but nevertheless it is true.

The pioneer walkers of the early rambling clubs were often members of the upper classes, with the time and money to dedicate to their pleasure. Their garb would be tweeds and breeches with the inevitable deerstalker hat. A little later, the railways brought the working classes to the hills with cloth caps and hobnailed boots, but still often with a jacket and usually a tie. The 1960s saw the growth of macho beards, heavy woollen sweaters, itchy woollen balaclavas and the pipe. Ex-army shops had an important influence on the wardrobe of most ramblers of this era, but fashions moved on and the growth in the number of outdoor equipment shops forced the retirement of the Navy flight-deck jacket, complete with earphone hoods, in favour of knee-length Helly Hanson cagoules.

It took several stages of evolution but now a mountain jacket and trousers in triple layer, windproof, waterproof and breathable material is available to any rambler, along with a rucksack full of electronic gadgets. Fashion aside, developments in fabric design and manufacturing techniques have been enormous and have made the modern-day hill-walking experience an altogether more comfortable and safer one. Yet it is strange to be able to look at any group photograph of mountaineers and realise that they are all wearing basically similar clothing and that the date of the image can be quite accurately guessed.

Clothing has always been the single most important piece of equipment taken on the hill. The human body is extremely adaptable and can tolerate the extreme cold or a soaking, but being cold and wet at the same time will soon cause the body to give up. This simple formula is known as 'exposure' and has caused the demise of many poor souls, but modern fabrics can play an important part in preventing the problem. The choice of equipment available to today's mountaineers is enormous – providing they have the money to match the price tag.

Mountain rescue teams traditionally work on a shoestring budget as the members have to raise the funds to cover team expenses. The cost of providing every team member with a complete set of clothes, boots, rucksack and all the other necessary personal gear is prohibitive and until recent times members provided all their own kit. Up to the 1980s a plastic armband supplied by the MRC was the only way of identifying someone as a rescue team member. However, in recent years most teams have started to issue some form of outer shell clothing so as to create a more professional image and to clearly identify team members to the public and other emergency services. Usually the purchase of such clothing is subsidised or sponsored by the manufacturer or supplier but the cost can still create a major hole in a team's budget.

TRANSPORT

The problems of transport in the mountain rescue world can be divided into two areas: getting people to the incident and getting equipment to the incident.

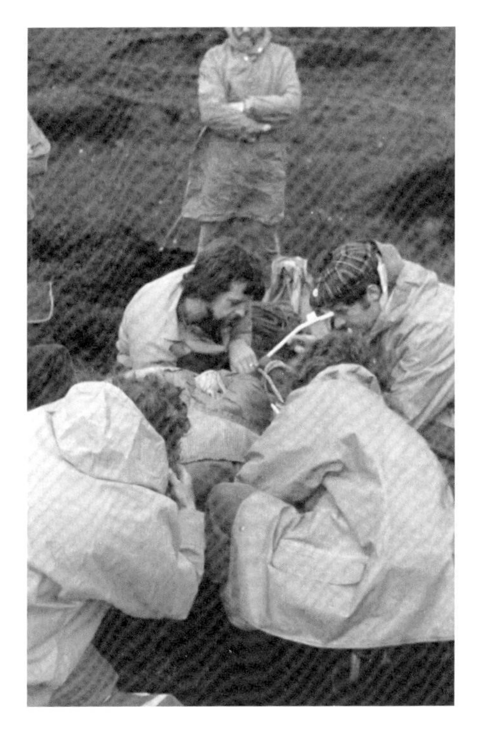

Above left: Members of Oldham MRT on exercise, sporting bright orange, knee-length cagoules, *c.*1971.

Top right: Oldham MRT gather at the back of its converted ambulance for a debrief after a call-out. Old ambulances were popular with rescue teams as they could be bought second-hand relatively cheaply or possibly even begged from the local ambulance service.

Above right: Another old ambulance with a new lease of life as a mountain rescue vehicle, this time parked outside Derby MRT's base for welcome maintenance.

Back in the 1930s and '40s personal transport was in short supply with only the wealthy few owning cars, but then local police officers, gamekeepers, shepherds and farmers would carry out most rescues. It was only when a search was necessary and outside help had to be sought that transport problems really arose. As previously mentioned, there are records of train and bus companies offering special deals to bona fide searchers travelling to places like Edale or Hayfield. The rail network, prior to the Beeching cuts, may have been more comprehensive than today but organising a search in the early days was never going to be a rushed affair.

Today a controller will try to choose a rendezvous point as close to an incident as possible but must also bear in mind the need for sufficient space for team members to park their vehicles. The members must get to that point quickly and most will simply drive directly there in their own vehicle. When the first rescue teams were being established in the 1960s personal car ownership was beginning to grow but many of the teams relied on youths or cadets too young to drive and transport for them must have been a headache.

In the 1960s and '70s teams still relied heavily on the equipment that was kept at MRC Rescue Posts and often the local PPPB Warden would be able to collect it in his Land Rover. Later, teams began to buy their own equipment and were forced to make all sorts of individual arrangements to transport it, which usually involved the stretcher being put in the back of a private car or van. Teams

Land Rovers are vehicles traditionally used by rescue teams all over the country, but Bleaklow peat stops even the RAF.

had very limited financial resources and buying a vehicle was a major decision. Buxton MRT was one of the first teams to acquire a vehicle, fondly christened 'The Pig', which spent as much time in the workshop as it did on the road, but was the team's pride and joy for several years.

Through the 1980s and '90s teams begged, bought and otherwise acquired a wide selection of vehicles that served their purposes at the time. However, as the service became more professional in its outlook some of the older vehicles were scrapped and teams embarked on massive fundraising campaigns to provide the cash to invest in newer vehicles. Blue lights and sirens began to appear from the mid-1990s to help combat the problem of moving through the growing volume of weekend traffic in the National Park.

The Land Rover is now the traditional choice of transport for mountain rescue teams as the versatility of the vehicle is difficult to match. Most teams own new, purpose-built or converted vehicles and the standard of their onboard equipment is comparable with the other emergency services. New regulations on construction and use of ambulances and blue light driving and recommendations from the MRC concerning livery mean that most rescue vehicles are now easily recognisble and present a more corporate and professional image. Like everything else, the downside of these improvements is the cost; a new, fully equipped mountain rescue vehicle is likely to cost in the region of £40,000.

MOUNTAIN RESCUE STRETCHERS

The problems of moving an injured casualty down a crag face or over rough terrain have always been the same. Any casualty, however trim their stature, soon becomes a heavy burden for rescuers to carry more than a few hundred metres. In the early days much improvisation was necessary and folklore tells of casualties being carried on beds made up from farm gates, rucksack frames, signposts and anything else that was freely to hand. Purpose-designed stretchers, like most mountain equipment, have inbuilt compromises between weight and strength and comfort and mobility.

Records show that the first RAF teams used folding canvas ambulance stretchers, but the shortcomings of these were soon realised and various homemade alternatives were often

A modern, two-piece Bell stretcher is correctly assembled standing on its end to ensure all the fittings are secure.

preferred. One stretcher available in the early days was known as the Neil Robertson stretcher and was designed in around 1910 for use in the confined space on ships. The stretcher was made of bamboo and canvas and a modern version is still manufactured today. One or two Peak District teams did acquire one of these stretchers but it is more allied to cave rescue and no record has been found of one ever actually being used on the hills.

The handbook published by the Mountain Rescue Committee in 1947 listed the equipment that may be available at Mountain Rescue Posts and included reference to a Duff stretcher, a Pigott stretcher and a Thomas stretcher.

The Duff stretcher was named after its designer, Donald Gordon Duff MBE MC FRCSE (1893–1968). Duff was a consultant at the hospital at Fort William and a pioneer in the Scottish mountain rescue world, being a founder member of Glencoe MRT and Lochaber MRT. The Duff stretcher was constructed from tubular steel with a folding mechanism making it easier to carry onto the hill. The stretcher also had leaf suspension and allowed for a wheel to be fitted underneath to ease the carry-down. The Duff was used in the Peak District in the early 1950s by a Derbyshire police team and is thought to be one of the first stretchers kept at Glossop Police Station. However, the Duff never really caught on in England and was always in the shadow of the more popular Thomas stretcher.

The Pigott Rope Stretcher is also listed in the 1947 MRC Handbook. This improvised stretcher is named after Alfred Pigott OBE who was a founder member of the MRC, chairman from 1956 to 1972 and president from 1972 to 1977. Alfred was a strong member of the Rucksack Club and lived in Cheadle Hulme near Stockport. His proximity to the Peak District meant he knew the area very well and he attended some of the early and formative meetings of the PPPB Voluntary Warden Team in 1956.

The Pigott stretcher is improvised from a climbing rope and it takes some practice to get the length of each loop and knot correct. The result is something resembling a rope ladder and it is very difficult to imagine just how a casualty of anything approaching adult weight could be carried on it for any distance. Also, the lack of support implicit in its design would have been very likely to aggravate any form of physical injury suffered by a casualty. The MRC later replaced the handbook information about the Pigott stretcher with instructions on tying an

Above left: Team members practise making a Pigott stretcher from a length of rope. It is hard to imagine the circumstances in which such an improvised stretcher would ever be used today.

Above right: Before lowering the stretcher it is always as well to make sure the patient is adequately fastened on. The team may have gone a little over the top here!

improvised 'Alpine Basket' from a single rope. The comfort of the casualty does not appear to have been much improved but he may have felt more secure cocooned in his personal knotted hammock. This is one stretcher design best left in the book.

Eustace Thomas and the Thomas Stretcher

The Thomas Stretcher is probably known to nearly every member of every mountain rescue team, although perhaps the younger members will not realise the significance of the designer's legacy to rescue in the UK. Eustace Thomas was born into a large family in 1869 and was brought up in London. He studied at Finsbury Technical College before moving to Manchester in 1900 to join his brother's company, Bertram Thomas (Engineers) Ltd. His interest in walking began whilst he still lived in London but it was road walking that became his passion when he moved to Manchester. He made three attempts at the Manchester to Blackpool Road Race with his best attempt – at the age of fifty – giving him third place with a time of nine hours and thirty minutes.

Thomas turned his attention to hill walking as a training exercise for his road walking. However, he was soon hooked and decided to attempt the Lakeland Fell Record. The route was to start and finish in Keswick and encompass as many summits as possible in twenty-four hours. In 1922, at the age of fifty-three, he set a new record of sixty-six and a half miles and 25,500ft of ascent. He then continued beyond the end of the specified twenty-four hours and added another thirteen miles and a further 4,500ft of ascent, until he had had enough after twenty-eight hours and thirty-five

Derby MRT shows off its equipment including a Thomas stretcher, a split Bell stretcher and a Neil Robertson stretcher (far left). Behind the Thomas stretcher are two drums fastened to back pack frames used to carry lowering rope to the top of a crag.

minutes. He joined the Alpine Club in 1923 and in 1928 became the first Englishman to climb all the eighty-three alpine peaks then known to be over 4,000 metres. In his early sixties he took up gliding and bought his own aeroplane, which he flew until the start of the war.

His contribution to mountain rescue came through his membership of the Rucksack Club, which he joined in 1909 and of which he was president in 1924 and 1925. The Rucksack Club, together with the Fell and Rock Club, formed the Joint Stretcher Committee in 1933 to look at designing a stretcher suitable for the rugged environment of mountain rescue. His design and engineering skills came to the fore, and along with the manufacturing capabilities of Bertram Thomas (Engineers) Ltd, he introduced the first Thomas stretcher.

The stretcher had an alloy construction which made it lightweight yet very robust. Long handles could be pulled out of the tubular frame to which web shoulder-yoke carrying straps were attached. Early versions had broad ash-wood runners to make sledging the stretcher a simpler option than carrying it, even on rock faces. Later versions replaced the canvas bed with a metal mesh bed and a redesign by Peter Bell in the 1960s allowed for the stretcher to be split in half, permitting it to be carried onto the hill by two people separately. The stretcher became the main piece of equipment supplied by the MRC and was to be found in nearly every rescue post in England and Wales for many years. The simple basic design was to last for over fifty years with only a few minor changes and it is likely that examples can still be found in many mountain rescue team bases today. Difficulties with manufacture during the late 1980s saw its demise and most teams in the Peak District turned instead to stretchers manufactured in the Lake District by Peter Bell. Eustace Thomas died in October 1960 aged ninety-one and despite his significant contribution to mountain rescue he was never officially recognised by the MRC.

Present-day Stretchers

Over the years all sorts of stretchers have found their way into the armoury of Peak District rescue teams. Before the days of regulations on load bearings, stress testing and so on, teams would acquire stretchers from whatever source they could if the price was right.

However, teams have become more aware of their responsibilities and of health and safety legislation. Consequently, all teams now use stretchers manufactured by responsible companies.

Following the demise of the Thomas, the Bell stretcher has become the standard for most teams. This stretcher is strong enough for the roughest terrain, including crag rescues, and its ability to split in half makes it easy to carry up the hill. The Lakeland manufacturer, Peter Bell, offers routine maintenance and stress test certification facilities, easing the conscience of team

Above left: A Thomas stretcher being used for the vertical lowering of a casualty using a single 'barrow boy' (rescuer guiding the stretcher). The Thomas was a sturdy stretcher very capable of taking the repeated beating of being dragged over rock. Note the net bag used to hold the casualty's feet and help give a reassuring feel of security for the patient. In practice a vertical lower can only be used for a limited type of injuries and a horizontal lower is normally preferred. However, a horizontal lower uses more equipment and takes longer to set up.

Top right: Eric Needham, vice chairman of Buxton MRT and proof-reader of this book, concentrates on negotiating a Thomas stretcher down a steep grass slope to a waiting casualty.

Above right: Ian Hurst checks the Thomas stretcher at the Roaches MRC rescue post, kept in a small out-building at Upper Hulme. Hanging on the wall behind him is a double Thomas leg splint and rucksacks containing first-aid equipment.

trustees. The MacInnes stretcher, originally designed by the famous Scottish mountaineer and rescuer Hamish MacInnes OBE BEM, is still favoured by several teams, whilst in the north of the PDMRO area Oldham MRT prefers the Alphin stretcher. The Alphin was designed and trialled by members of Oldham team in conjunction with the safety equipment manufacturer, Troll. It is a narrow, folding stretcher with a laminated bed, ideal for use on crags and light in weight for easier carrying up the hill.

MEDICAL CARE

The first MRC Handbook, published in 1947, lists the standard mountain first-aid equipment that should be available at a rescue post. This list is comprehensive and includes many of the

MacInnes stretcher designed by Hamish MacInnes from the Glencoe MRT.

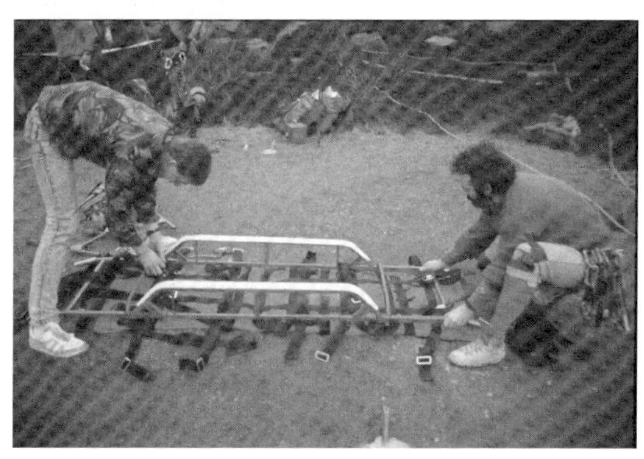

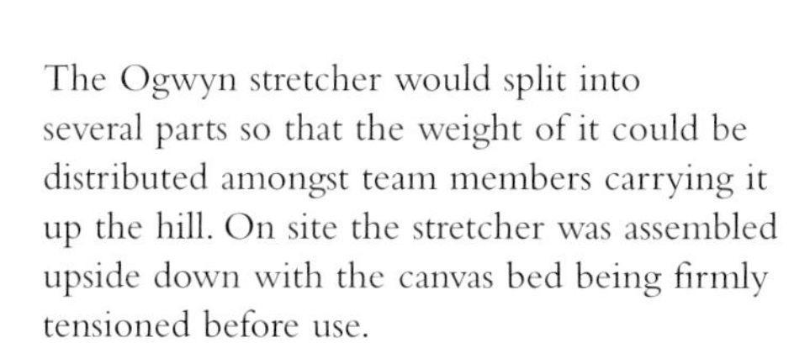

The Ogwyn stretcher would split into several parts so that the weight of it could be distributed amongst team members carrying it up the hill. On site the stretcher was assembled upside down with the canvas bed being firmly tensioned before use.

Practising with an Alphin stretcher rigged for a horizontal lower. Normally the stretcher would be folded on the back of one of the rescuers who would descend until it was level with the casualty. The stretcher would then be opened out to its full length and the casualty lowered onto the bed using a pulley device. Here members are about to descend over the edge of a crag in Cheedale and are getting familiar with the Alp lowering devices which permit the descent to be controlled by the barrow boys (rescuers attached to the stretcher).

standard wound dressings and bandages that are still carried today. The difference between then and now would be the weight of each item and its cost.

Caring for an injured casualty is fundamental to the aims of mountain rescue. A rescue team may initially have to treat serious injuries and then have to care for the patient for a number of hours until the stretcher arrives at the road-head. Whilst basic dressings may have stayed the same the development of peripheral equipment has moved on almost beyond recognition. As with all mountain-use equipment there is usually a compromise between functionality and practicality, but there are now several manufacturing companies specialising in field casualty products and they have greatly advanced the design of rescue equipment.

Shelter is often the first priority at a casualty site but breathable lightweight fabrics such as Gore-Tex have long since replaced the old heavy canvas tents. The treatment of nearly every

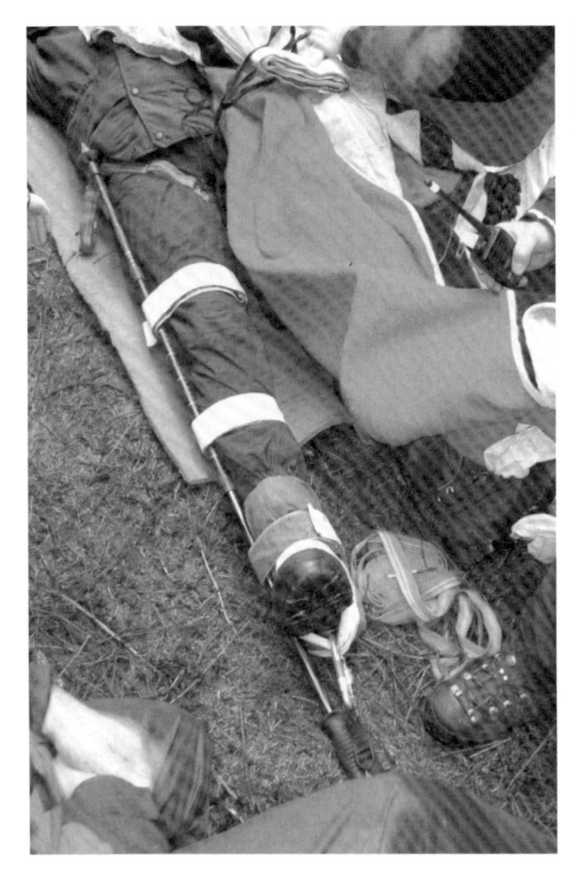

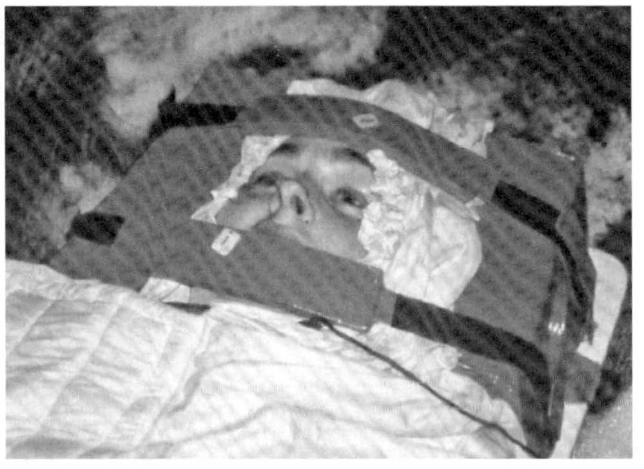

Above: Team members practise making an improvised leg traction splint from a walking pole, tape slings and a karabiner. Not recommended practice when responding as a rescue team but in an emergency situation it could help reduce pain and shock in a casualty when help is still some hours away.

Left: Back injuries are common in climbing accidents and teams do all they can to ensure the casualty is correctly splinted to prevent further damage to the spine during transportation. For short duration evacuations a casualty is placed on a backboard fitted with restraining pads which prevent any head or neck movement.

casualty will now start with the application of oxygen, but gone are the heavy iron bottles which have been replaced by lightweight, high-pressure ones with double the capacity. Morphine has been available to rescue teams since 1935 but now a team can offer a small range of analgesics, each simply packaged and ready for use. The condition of the casualty can now be continuously monitored during the carry-off to ensure that the patient is handed over to the ambulance or hospital staff in the best possible condition.

Mountain rescue in the Peak District has been fortunate to have the good support of local doctors, paramedics and the ambulance service in developing its treatment and care package. Casualty care is now a far cry from that offered in the 1960s and is set to become more and more sophisticated.

Opposite below: Medical Anti-Shock Trousers, or Mast suit for short, were introduced from America in the early 1990s and were a product of the Vietnam war. The theory was that gentle pressure was applied to the legs and lower abdominal area in order to counteract a drop in a casualty's blood pressure following an accident. The trousers were slowly pumped up to specific levels measured by the first aider on gauges attached to the suit. Whilst the theory may have been sound, in practice the suit was difficult to manage and fit. Moreover, hospital casualty staff were not familiar with the device and as incorrect deflation of the suit could cause a sudden and serious drop in blood pressure, the suit was withdrawn from service in the Peak District before it had ever been used on a real casualty.

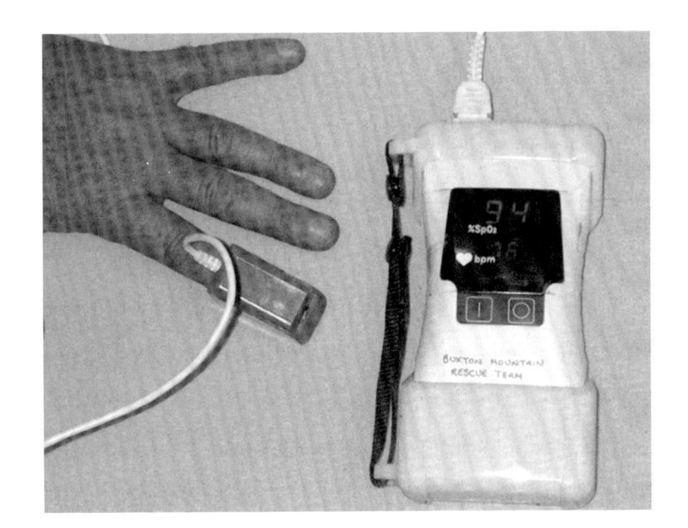

A modern addition to the rescuer's casualty care kit is the Pulse Oximeter, a robust and lightweight gadget which indicates the oxygen saturation level of the casualty and the pulse rate.

In the early 1970s Glossop MRT was called to Loftend Quarry above Crowden where a large flake of rock had fallen, crushing a youth below. Dr Derek Bunting, team doctor (third from the left) attended and set up what is thought to be the first intravenous fluid drip used by mountain rescue in the Peak Disrict. His actions worked and despite severe internal injuries the casualty survived to tell the tale.

Above left: Loftend Quary, *c.*1970. This large flake had come away from the quarry face and crushed the casualty. Disused quarries appear to offer the perfect climbing environment but in actual fact can be extremely dangerous places. Blasting of the rock face when the quarry was working will have caused cracks in the rock. Water and frost permeate the cracks and the result can be a rock face which, deceptively, looks tempting but in fact is very unstable.

Above right: Ray Davies (Glossop Team Leader) tries one of the new Pye Bantam portable radios obtained by the PDMRO in the mid-1960s. The radios were early transistor technology and were famous for wandering off their allocated frequency. Situated in the north of the Peak District, on Black Hill, is the Holmes Moss television transmitter and teams working in this area had to put up with the BBC Light Radio Station constantly interfering with reception. Note the very long whip aerial attached to the radio, a nuisance to carry and a danger to other members. Ray Davies was recognised in Her Majesty's New Year's Honours in 2007 with the MBE for services to mountain rescue.

THE RESCUE BASE

As teams began to be more formally organised they acquired equipment and vehicles and the need for a permanent base or headquarters arose. In the true tradition of mountain rescue all sorts of buildings were acquired, often with rents and expenses waived by their generous landlords. However, in the endless pursuit of professionalism, some of the older buildings were eventually deemed no longer big enough or possibly safe enough to permit their continued occupation.

Purchasing land and erecting a purpose-designed building involves massive expense and some recent constructions in other regions have cost many hundreds of thousands of pounds. The ethics of spending such sums of donated money is debatable but fortune has saved the Peak District teams from such expenditure. Each of the seven teams in the Peak has a base

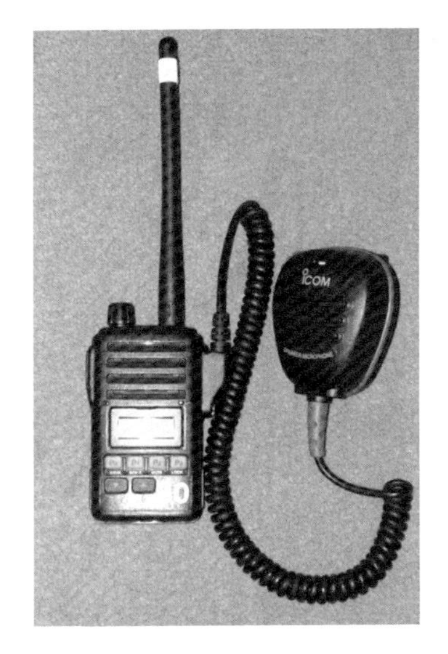

Above left: The latest radios issued by the police to Peak District mountain rescue teams. Light, waterproof, and capable of receiving multiple frequencies, allowing each team to use its own individual channel whilst remaining in contact with others during a multi-team incident. Compare the size of aerial!

Above right: The upper room of Buxton's old base in Dove Holes quarry following renovation and decoration. This was a small building but – at the time – adequate with the central roof beams often used for training.

suitable for its requirements and most rely on the generosity of a landlord. Two teams, perhaps appropriately, rely on breweries and the others on commercial companies. Buxton team's base, the only purpose-built one, could not have been erected without the free lease of the land from a local community association. Edale MRT, the latest team to move, now has a newly renovated building with a purpose-designed interior, courtesy of a quarrying company. Whilst the cost of the renovation was borne by the team it still could not have completed its transfer without the help of the company.

Such is the support that mountain rescue in the Peak District receives from local businesses, that it is difficult to imagine how it would operate without it. Mountain rescue is recognised as a community service and is grateful for the generous support that the community offers in return.

HELICOPTERS

One of the most important changes in mountain rescue has been the development of helicopters and their adaptation to rescue work. Helicopters are complicated and expensive machines to operate and until relatively recently mountain rescue had to rely solely on the aircraft of the RAF for support in the hills. Whilst the RAF helicopters are maintained primarily for rescue of HM Forces personnel they have played a strategic role in civilian rescue since 1955 when the Westland Whirlwind aircraft was first formally adapted for search and rescue and took on the now familiar bright yellow paint scheme.

An RAF Westland Whirlwind helicopter waiting at Crowden during a search of Longdendale during 1977. Despite the Whirlwind being in service since 1955 as a search and rescue helicopter the first mountain rescue incident involving the lift of a casualty is claimed to have been during 1960 when a fallen climber was rescued from Ossian's Cave in Glencoe, Scotland. The first use of a helicopter in the Peak District is not certain but it is known that an RAF Whirlwind was deployed to search for a missing aircraft in 1963 and was used again during the 1964 Four Inns search of Bleaklow.

After the availability of radios, the introduction of helicopters is probably the most important development in mountain rescue to date. The Whirlwind was only a small aircraft compared to the modern Sea King but it had the capability of winching a casualty out of awkward situations and transporting them smoothly to hospital within minutes.

Helicopters can offer three types of assistance. They provide an aerial platform from which it is far easier to search for a missing person or to identify the exact position of a casualty. They can provide a fast means of transport for rescue personnel from the valley to the hilltop, and they provide a fast and smooth method of getting a casualty from the mountain to a hospital.

The RAF aircraft supporting the Peak District rescue teams are normally from 'E' Flight 202 Squadron, based at RAF Leconfield at Beverley in the East Riding of Yorkshire. The squadron now operates the Westland Sea King helicopter and can be off base and flying over the Peak District within thirty-five minutes. The Sea King first entered service with the RAF search and rescue squadrons in 1977 but was not based at Leconfield until 1992. It is a large aircraft measuring 17m in length, with a rotor diameter of nearly 19m. The aircraft can operate for up to six and a half

Above left: The introduction of helicopters also brought dangers to the rescuers on the ground. Regular training was quickly arranged to introduce team members to the problems that the down-draught of the rotors can cause and to teach the correct and safe methods of approaching an aircraft. The annual team helicopter exercise was, and still is, always well attended!

Above right: From the mid-1960s the RAF started to introduce the larger Westland Wessex helicopter into the search and rescue squadrons. The Wessex had a greater carrying capacity and was capable of longer operations.

hours without refuelling, which is particularly useful in a search situation. Its two Rolls-Royce engines give it sufficient power to enable it to operate in the severest weather conditions but they, and its five-blade rotors, also produce a considerable down-draught which can be hazardous to team members on the ground. However, the size of the aircraft offers two main advantages in the rescue situation. Apart from its four crew members, one of which is trained to paramedic standard, the Sea King can carry up to nineteen passengers, enabling a large proportion of a team to be lifted and deployed in one sortie. The main advantage of the Sea King is its ability to operate with a winch which permits aerial rescues from the most awkward locations.

Another source of aerial assistance is The North Midlands Helicopter Support Unit based at Derbyshire Police Headquarters at Ripley. This is a police helicopter that can be over the remotest part of the Peak District within minutes. Whilst its role is primarily police duties, being equipped with a heat-seeking device enables it to be of great assistance in the search situation and to act as a communications platform. Its role in rescue is limited but in desperate circumstances the aircraft can carry a casualty if some of the seats are removed. Other surrounding police forces can offer similar helicopter assistance and Cheshire Constabulary operates a small fixed-wing aircraft for searching.

This Wessex helicopter has just landed below Hayfield Reservoir to unload an exercise casualty. The fuselage of the aircraft was quite low giving easy access to the main door, but the proximity of the large exhaust situated under the pilot's position could quickly dry your hair!

A Westland Sea King helicopter approaches for landing on the moor. The Sea King search and rescue helicopter operated by the RAF came into service in 1977; however, it wasn't regularly seen in the Peak District until the mid-1990s when the last of the Wessex aircraft was replaced.

Of much more practical assistance are the helicopters of the County Air Ambulance Service. Although these aircraft can only fly during daylight and have no winching facility, they are small and able to land in very confined areas. The Peak District is served by several air ambulances and one can normally be over an incident site within twenty minutes of a call. The aircraft are usually crewed by a pilot and two paramedics, enabling ongoing casualty care from the hilltop to hospital.

Whilst helicopters are marvellous tools for transporting patients to hospital they will never totally replace the rescue teams. Weather conditions and other contingencies often dictate the availability of a helicopter, which can be delayed or prevented from attending the incident for all sorts of reasons. Even with an aircraft available it is normally still the task of the rescue team to carry the casualty to the nearest landing site. Safety is always the key issue and rescue team members are required to take on special training before they are allowed to work in or around the aircraft.

NINE

TRAINING

Devoting time to training is a key element of being a member of any modern rescue team. Most training is delivered in-house by senior team members who pass on their knowledge and practical experience to others. Each team sets its own standards, broadly in line with those of its neighbours within the region. Following this traditional format keeps costs low and only for very special subjects has there been a need to bring in outside speakers. Records from the 1950s recall major training exercises involving 100 or more searchers sweeping the moors; whether anything was learnt from these events is difficult to say but teams now have a rather more considered approach and topics are first covered in the classroom before being exercised on the hill. Mountain rescue will always have an element of danger and quality training will reduce the risk of another accident occurring. Personal safety is paramount, followed by an awareness of the need to protect the safety of everyone else involved. Training has to be constructive, interesting and fun if volunteers are to keep volunteering because the average member will spend at least four times the hours on training than responding to call-outs.

Training is what makes the difference between a group of individuals and a team. There is a myriad of skills to be acquired if a new entrant is to become an efficient team member and team training officers ponder long and hard on how to fit all the necessary subjects into an annual programme. The correct topics have to be identified, researched and delivered in a quality and timely manner to students with varying levels of natural ability and experience – no easy task, especially when dealing with a group of volunteers with a limited amount of free time to devote.

It is for this reason that most teams are particularly selective when it comes to recruiting members because, whilst teams will teach the technicalities of rescue, they expect the recipient to be already experienced in mountaineering. It is that basic experience of being at one with the fundamentals of exploring the great outdoors that is such an important element of being a successful and safe rescuer. The basic skill is known as hill-craft and there are no short cuts to learning it. Books, courses and videos are helpful but there is no better teacher than experience and that only comes the hard way. Within hill-craft come the finer skills of navigation, weather awareness, clothing selection, route finding, pace setting, nutrition intake, escape route planning and above all else, an appreciation of the natural beauties, wonders and dangers of the hills. A sound knowledge of hill-craft encourages respect for all aspects of the mountains and mountaineering without which a person may become a liability to himself and others. Little wonder then that the average age of members in most rescue teams is well in the forties.

Reflecting on the early days of Peak District mountain rescue, when scout and cadet groups played such an important part in forming teams, it is difficult to believe that they would have had much experience of hill-craft. Perhaps enthusiasm, fitness and the self-confident invincibility of youth saved the day. However, it is noticeable that none of today's teams are still directly connected to youth movements.

CASUALTY CARE

The 1964 Four Inns tragedy brought a rude awakening to many in the outdoor world about the apparent lack of knowledge relating to mountain hypothermia, or exposure as it used to be called. It seems unbelievable today that there was not more awareness of such a basic cause of death on the hills but it perhaps reflects that outdoor pursuit training was still in its infancy and only a few special centres had yet been established.

Several leading names in the medical world, some with mountain experience, had produced papers on the causes, symptoms and treatment of exposure but there seems to have been a general lack of public awareness. Ralph Blain, Chief Instructor of the Ullswater Outward Bound School in the Lake District, had produced one report which referred to an earlier paper produced by Dr D.G. Duff who was involved in Scottish mountain rescue. Another paper was produced by Dr L.G.C.E. Pugh who was a Medical Research Council scientist and who had been involved with experiments into the effects of extreme environments on the human physiology. He had accompanied the 1953 British Everest Expedition and is credited with solving many of their high altitude problems and so contributing greatly to the success of the expedition. Following the Four Inns incident a number of the Derby Rover Scouts assisted in practical experiments with Dr Pugh. These included swallowing an electronic thermometer (a Wolf Temperature Pill) to determine the change of inner and outside body temperature during prolonged exercise. Apparently, 10*s* was paid for the recovery and return of the thermometer to the Medical Research Institute, so there was probably no shortage of volunteers.

Publicity following the Four Inns did a lot to highlight the dangers of hypothermia and in November 1964 the British Mountaineering Council published a booklet, *Exposure*, explaining its dangers; another legacy from the three scouts lost in the March of that year.

First-aid teaching in most teams had traditionally relied on a syllabus set out by one of the major names in first aid, such as St John Ambulance or The Red Cross. However, it had long been recognised that first aid in the mountain rescue situation needed something extra, as it was inevitable that there was always going to be a delay in getting the casualty to hospital. Dr Ieuan Jones of the Bangor Hospital in North Wales was one of the first to format a syllabus especially for the rescue situation in the 1960s and it particularly concentrated on the benefits of a good examination and diagnosis. Through the 1980s and '90s the MRC approached both St John and The Red Cross to use their resources to develop a course but the negotiations faltered and the MRC resolved to go it alone. Casualty care is a fascinatingly complicated subject and a difficult one for a group of volunteers to reformat and publish as a syllabus but this was finally achieved in 2000. The MRC Casualty Care Course is now the accepted standard in all mountain rescue teams and up to 25 per cent of a team's training time will be spent on it.

CRAG RESCUE

The rescue of someone injured and trapped on a cliff face is the worst-case scenario for any rescue team. In wilder, more mountainous parts of Britain, the task may be even more complicated by the remoteness of the crag, the length of the pitch and the weather at high altitude. Fortunately, in the Peak District most of the crags are not too far from the road, which is probably what makes them some of the most popular climbing edges in the country. The sheer number of people who participate in the sport on these edges means that the incidence of rock-climbing accidents is higher there than anywhere else in the UK. There are over 10,000 named climbs listed in the various Peak District climbing guidebooks, on both gritstone and

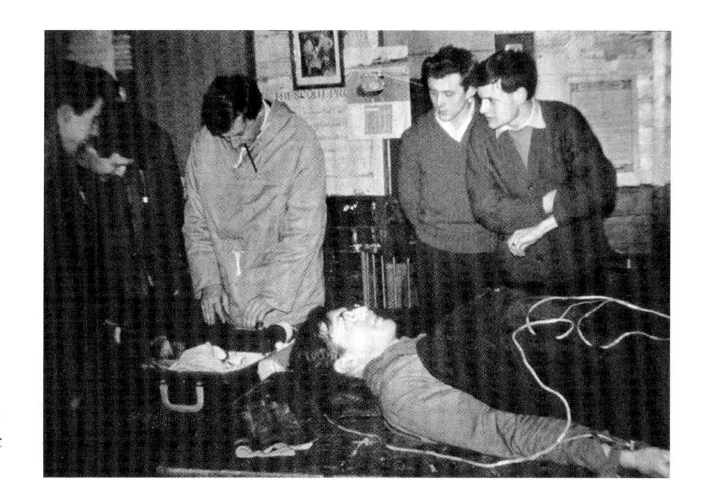

Dr Pugh starts his hypothermia trials on willing members of Derby Rover Scout MRT which involved swallowing an electronic thermometer.

A Derby scout all wrapped up in a foam rubber insulation suit, part of Dr Pugh's trials and investigations into dealing with hypothermia.

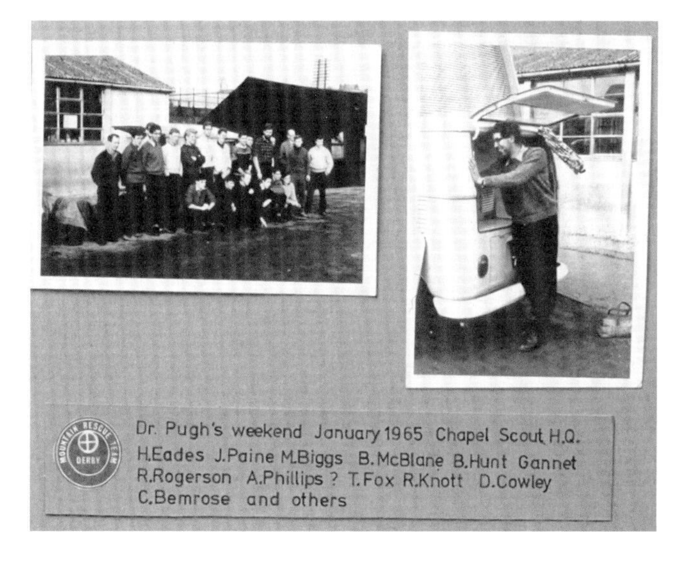

An image taken from a display board showing two photographs of the small group who took the challenge of Dr Pugh to swallow the electronic thermometer.

limestone, and on a summer weekend literally hundreds of people can be seen on some of the more famous edges such as Stanage or the Roaches.

Whilst the number of rock-climbing accidents is high in the Peak District, the rather cynical – but nevertheless fortunate – aspect from a rescue point of view, is that because of the nature of the crags most casualties will have hit the ground. A casualty lying on the ground, no matter how badly injured, is far easier to deal with than one suspended by a thread 30m up. However, with some of the limestone crags in the region reaching up to 100m high it is inevitable that from time to time an aerial rescue requiring the use of ropes will be needed.

Rope has always been on every rescue team's equipment list but the older ropes were stiff and particularly heavy, especially when they got wet. Rope design and manufacture has improved over the years and the older hemp and hawser laid ropes have given way to modern, pre-stretched nylon ropes that are much more lightweight and water resistant. However, it is only in relatively recent years that equipment has been designed especially for rescue work.

Traditionally rescuers adapted standard climbing hardware such as karabiners to meet their needs. However, with the modern-day alertness to risk awareness, proper testing and measuring of the loads and stresses placed on a system have become the norm. There was some consternation when it was discovered that the loads applied to equipment during a rescue attempt far exceeded the manufacturer's limits and thus new designs and ideas were needed. There was never a shortage of ideas and new gadgets have been regularly coming on to the market for several years.

Teams have traditionally designed their own crag rescue and lowering systems, usually with the help of the active climbers within the membership and with reference to such books as *The RAF Mountain Rescue Handbook* and *The International Mountain Rescue Handbook*, written by Hamish MacInnes. Oldham MRT took the problem a stage further and developed their system around a home-grown lowering device known as the Alp. The traditional systems usually work with the stretcher being lowered from above whereas the Oldham system uses fixed ropes with the lower being controlled by the 'barrow boys' (rescuers handling the stretcher as it is lowered).

A rescue system simlar to those using 'barrow boys', but here the stretcher and lower are being controlled from the ground.

Above: The Clog Figure of Eight abseil device has been regularly used as a method of controlling a stretcher lower. The device was never designed for such practice and this photograph shows the excessive wear that can occur after repeated misuse. As teams began to pay more attention to the stresses and loads that were being applied to equipment during rescues, various purposely designed devices began to appear. Oldham MRT was one of the first to help develop a special lowering device, known as the Alp. The Alp permitted the rescuer to control his own rate of descent rather than being lowered by another person from overhead. The Alp is still in common use but many other similar devices with 'dead-man' safety handles are now prevalent in many teams.

Right: Team members practise rigging an aerial ropeway. A technique of limited use in the Peak District, but one that allows the stretcher and casualty to be lowered from the crag avoiding the boulder field underneath. Careful calculation of the load and stress on the rope and anchors needs to be considered before attempting this system.

In the new millennium Mountain Rescue (England and Wales) supported a fresh look at lowering systems and encouraged a technique known as Rigging for Rescue. The technique prompts teams to examine existing systems and ask themselves, 'What if…?' and basically encourages the use of a back-up system for each aspect of the lowering procedure. It is not without its critics as some would see it as making a science from an otherwise simple procedure, and the use of additional ropes makes the job more complicated and more expensive. However, in recent years teams have been adopting at least some of the new ideas and Rigging for Rescue is quickly becoming the national standard.

Training and preparing for a crag evacuation is a lengthy and costly business with the emphasis always on safety. In the Peak District the necessity for an aerial stretcher evacuation is a rare event but mountain rescue has to be equipped and skilled to carry out the task and this readily justifies the commitment and expenditure.

A mock casualty is lowered down Red Wall at Holyhead into a waiting inshore lifeboat. There is a calm sea on this occasion, but this is a tricky job when the lifeboat is rising and falling on the swell.

Meeting and training with other regions and services helps the development of new ideas. Teams from the Peak District regularly send members on a course held by HM Coastguard at Holyhead on Anglesey. The sea cliffs near to Holyhead are renowned as some of the best climbing routes in the country and part of the local coastguard has formed a sea cliff rescue team. The course covers the many different aspects of rescue that members of Peak district teams would not normally experience such as rocket line firing and the use of lifeboats.

SEARCHING

Looking for the walker who has failed to return from a day in the hills has been the staple diet of rescue teams since their inception. Indeed, within the Peak District, it was the need to create a search facility that was the driving factor in the formation of most of the teams. A sweep search was the usual method in the early days and meant getting as many people as possible to line out just a few yards apart and then to walk on a set compass bearing until someone came to

Huddersfield Rover Scout Team line out for a sweep search in winter conditions. In the early days, before radios were available, the speed and direction of the line would be controlled using whistles or flags. Even with radio communication it takes a lot of training to establish the self-discipline required to maintain a straight line and to ensure the searchers do not get so far apart that a small area is missed. Before helicopters and search dogs this was the only method of being sure that the target of the search was not in the area. It is a very slow and painstaking method that requires a lot of people and sustained concentration.

an obstacle. It always was a tricky method, especially when there may have been 100 people in the line and not everyone could afford a compass. Without radios to help control direction and speed, progress must have been slow and ragged.

In the late 1960s, Fred Heardman, landlord of the Nag's Head at Edale, created search maps of Kinder Scout and Bleaklow Moor by sectioning the land into easily manageable portions and giving every portion a unique number. A smaller searching party could then be directed to go and scour that particular area, making control of the whole search so much easier. It was the start of a search management system that, in a revised form, is still favoured today.

The need for major searches of the moors has reduced over the years with the introduction of much-improved maps, more way-marked paths and better navigation equipment. However, the Peak District teams are still called to search incidents fairly regularly and then the result of a lot of classroom training and field exercises will be put to the test.

Training for searches has to be provided at two levels. The team member needs to understand the importance of a thorough search without wasting time and there are several methods that can be applied, depending on circumstances. The search controller must elicit as much relevant information as possible from the reporter of the incident and then needs the skill to format a search pattern of the areas where the casualty is most likely to be. The now common use of mobile telephones often permits a lost person to speak directly from the hill to the search controller. The controller will ask the lost person for a description of the surrounding terrain and may be able to use his detailed local knowledge of the area to guide the person verbally to safety.

The controller needs a thorough knowledge of the area and the experience to be able to make best use of all the resources at his disposal, including search dogs and helicopters, as well as the teams. Learning these skills is a matter of practice, experience and of making use of data from previous searches in similar circumstances. However, on the hill, it is still the eyes and ears of the team members that get results.

Key factors to any search operation are good control and record keeping, which can only be attained through quality and regular training. Depicted here is the mountain rescue search control room of a major search in North Wales in November 1988. North Wales's teams had called for the assistance of Peak District teams to search for a young schoolgirl named Anna Humphries. The teams spent several days combing farmland and the result of each part of the search was carefully recorded on the control map to ensure no area was missed or repeatedly searched. Entering data onto the map is Ted Burton (Buxton MRT) and seated far right is Tony Jones, a search controller from North Wales. Anna Humphries had in fact been abducted and murdered, and although her body was eventually found well outside the initial search area, some of her belongings and other related evidence were found by the teams and recovered by the police. The offender was captured in France and received a life sentence.

The same principles of incident control management are needed on every event. Here Dave Crossland and Barry Gregory manage a Woodhead MRT incident from the back of a trailer. As with most things in mountain rescue economy is the driving force, but a simple trailer fitted with a radio and a map table gives adequate shelter in order to control the average incident with relative comfort. With no expense spared facilities have been further enhanced with the provision of refreshment and welfare equipment (gas ring and kettle).

Training and working on the moors is normal practise for rescue teams but sometimes the real call-out asks for more unpleasant tasks to be performed. Here teams sweep search Glossop Council refuse tip in a search for a young boy named Shaun Bonner whose body was later found in a pool nearby.

The Peak District lies under the flight-path of one of the country's busiest airports – Manchester. The possibility of a major aircraft incident may be remote but cannot be totally discounted and the use of mountain rescue teams is included in the emergency plans for such an event. Teams regularly visit the airport and train with the fire brigade to learn the procedures for safe access to aircraft and appreciate the inherent dangers of a modern aircraft wreck.

Working in the confined space of an aircraft, members quickly realise that the emergency exits are not made for conventional mountain rescue stretchers and here the team practises using a Paraguard stretcher.

Following the Lockerbie air disaster of Pan Am flight 103 in December 1988 Peak District teams joined the local police and other teams from around the country to help in a search for evidence and property belonging to the 270 fatalities. Debris was blown and scattered over a huge area in the mid-air explosion.

THE FUTURE

The importance of individual and team training was recognised by the PDMRO very early on, and so, too, was the need for a levelling of standard practice across the member teams thought necessary. In November 1972 the first training course for team leaders was organised by Vin Machin of the Glossop team and held at Crowden Youth Hostel. The three-day course cost a princely £3 per head and was aimed at existing and aspiring leaders. Its purpose was to demonstrate some of the specialist rescue techniques already in use by certain teams and to highlight and enhance the skills required for organising a search. The whole of the Saturday night was dedicated to a search exercise in Crowden Great Brook. This course was the forerunner of similar training events to be organised annually by the PDMRO that continue to educate both novice and experienced members of the organisation to this day. The involvement of both students and instructors from outside the region has helped provide a crossover of ideas and continues to stimulate the development of mountain rescue as a whole.

The expectations of the modern team are such that every member needs to be competent in a range of skills beyond hill-craft. Just being experienced in a subject is no longer good enough and there is a growing culture of needing to hold the correct certificate before a skill may be deployed. The slide to certification started back in 1971 when the rules for Initial Operation Team status demanded that 25 per cent of a team's membership had to be trained in first aid. First aid in mountain rescue went out of the window many years ago and was replaced by 'casualty care', covering everything from basic resuscitation to administering controlled drugs. In order to provide this standard of care and be covered under the necessary insurance policy each member must now hold a Casualty Care Certificate, renewable every three years as a minimum.

Hamish MacInnes, in his introduction to *The International Rescue Handbook*, says, 'Professional [i.e. paid, full-time] groups will by necessity evolve.' Certainly the low budget, self-help ethos of volunteers doing their best to help other like-minded outdoor enthusiasts is slowly being eroded. There is a danger of it being replaced by highly qualified rescue practitioners, knowledgeable in all the technicalities of mountain rescue, but afraid that using improvisation and stepping outside the excepted standard practice will leave them open to criticism or possibly litigation. In fairness, the casualty today receives far better treatment on the hill than ever before, but where will the line be drawn? There is only so much that a volunteer can do in his spare time and it will be a sad day when an enthusiastic team member is barred from helping other hill-goers for the want of a certificate.

TEN

OPERATIONS

When the radio pager goes off on a Sunday afternoon it is quite likely to be calling the team to one of a regular list of incidents – a fallen climber, a walker with a leg injury, a paraglider who has landed heavily or a mountain biker who went downhill more quickly than his bike. However, just occasionally, the teams are called to more unusual incidents.

DOGS

In January 1986 Kinder Team was called to Crowden Head, the very summit of Kinder Scout, where a very large Old English Sheepdog named Henry had collapsed from a suspected heart attack. PPPB part-time ranger staff tried for some time to coax the dog and its distressed owner off the hill but eventually it was decided to call Kinder Mountain Rescue Team. Henry was placed on the stretcher and the evacuation commenced down to Hayfield. The carry-off lasted well into the dark hours but eventually both dog and owner were reunited and Henry made a full recovery.

INDUSTRY

At 8.30 p.m. on 11 January 2003 Buxton Team was called to Tunstead Quarry, Buxton, following the report of a climber 'crag fast on the quarry wall'. How the report became so twisted has never been resolved, as in fact the call was to assist a quarry worker who had been carrying out maintenance on a large cement silo and had fallen fifty feet into the empty hopper.

There followed a multi-service rescue where the mountain rescue team set up a rope system to lower East Midlands Ambulance paramedic, Tom Bailey, and team member, Andy Humberstone, into the silo. The fire service set up additional lighting and then provided the muscle to pull the rescuers and the casualty back out again. Despite horrific injuries the maintenance worker made a full recovery.

WATER

In September 2000 Glossop and Woodhead teams were called to the aid of two young boys trapped by rising river water in an area known as the Blacks, near Woodhead Tunnel off the A628. By the time the teams arrived the boys were in serious trouble as flash flooding had caused the river to rise dramatically in a very short time. The team had no special clothing or equipment to deal with the situation and had had no previous training or experience. Team members bravely faced the white water and managed to reach and rescue the two boys.

This event highlighted a major gap in rescue team training. The whole aspect of team members working in or by water was risk assessed and a plan was developed to equip and train some members in water safety. Whilst the organisation is not orientated towards rescue from

A cartoon by 'Mick' printed in the *Peak Park News* in late 1986 portrays the events on Kinder in January when Henry the Old English sheepdog had to be carried down to Hayfield by the Kinder MRT.

The Star, Monday, September 25, 2000

LOCAL NEWS

Schoolboys saved from raging torrent

A newspaper cutting from *The Star* showing members of Glossop MRT and Woodhead MRT desperately trying to cross the river to reach the two frightened boys. This rescue was to have a considerable impact on future training in the Peak District.

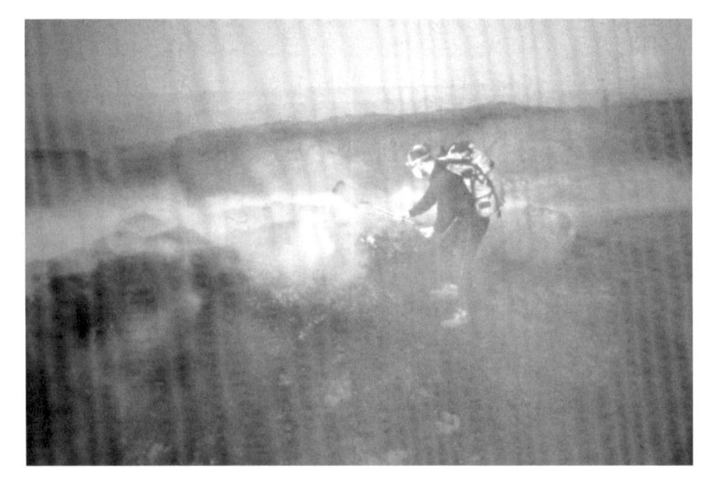

Without any special equipment other than a paper face mask team members attempt to beat out the fires which attack the moors every year.

moving water it is now correctly equipped and trained to protect its own members whilst searching or working near water.

FIRES

Another task not readily associated with mountain rescue is that of firefighting. Until recent times PDMRO teams were regularly tasked to help the fire service and landowners to extinguish moorland fires. Most of the upper moors have a good covering of heather which, in spring, will be home to many different breeds of ground nesting birds. The woody heather soon dries out in the sun and a discarded cigarette or the magnifying effect of broken glass can soon cause it to ignite. The results can be devastating, destroying not just the vegetation but any nests in its path. If the ground is still moist then the heather will regenerate but if the fire has been hot enough to get into the peat itself then the heather roots are damaged and can no longer hold the peat together. The result is that the remaining peat dries out and blows away on the wind leaving huge areas of barren land and bedrock. Moorland may never recover from such a severe fire.

Fighting Moorland fires is a dirty and dangerous job but one which team members volunteered to do in order to save their precious landscapes and its wildlife habitats. However, in the 1990s the Peak District Fires Operations Group was established and risk assessed moorland firefighting activities. It was decided that the mountain rescue volunteer was being placed at undue risk which their training and equipment did not mitigate and that fires were better tackled by experts in the subject. A great deal of planning and money went into forming a strategy to deal with fires as soon as they are reported and before they can get a good hold on the ground. That strategy involves the use of helicopters to lift water from local reservoirs and dump hundreds of gallons directly onto the fire. A far more effective method than a man beating the flames with an old bit of rubber conveyor belt nailed to a stick. Mountain rescue team members were not disappointed to be left out of the strategy!

SHEEP

Someone once said that it is impossible for a human being to walk past a sheep without saying 'baa' to it. However, different expletives have often been issued by rescue team members to the sheep allegedly stuck on a crag face. Sheep stuck on rock faces is not an uncommon report but often, if left for a day or two, the sheep's hunger improves its confidence and it will usually find its own way out of difficulty. Only when the same sheep has been in the same position for a few days will rescue teams put members at risk to save the animal.

A CRIME SCENE?

In 2005 a small number of Buxton team members went to the assistance of Derbyshire police officers who were concerned by the wreckage of a motor vehicle precariously positioned high up on a ledge of a recently disused quarry. The police needed to gain access to the vehicle to identify it and to ensure there was nobody was still in it. As a potential crime scene the team rigged ropes and safety lines to enable the officers to climb to the vehicle. Fortunately the vehicle was empty and it was presumed that it had been pushed off the top of the quarry by joyriders.

This lonely ewe has been on the ledge for a few days.

Team members are lowered to the ledge.

The sheep, safely in the bag, is lowered to the ground.

Buxton team fixes ropes and safety lines to assist police officers to access the scene.

This squashed car looked as though it had been through a roller press

Peak District teams have assisted the police at many crime scenes and have had the grim task of recovering several bodies from situations that have nothing to do with mountaineering. However, the teams acknowledge that they have special skills that can be useful in extraordinary circumstances and members are happy to assist when called.

ELEVEN

THEN AND NOW: A SUMMARY

An injured walker or climber in the 1930s may have had to wait hours just for the report of his accident to reach anyone in authority. If he was fortunate, the local bobby would have had enough contacts to gather together a small band of people to return to the scene with a blanket and a field dressing; the carry-off may then have taken many more hours. Now, with the touch of a few buttons, a whole organisation can swing into action bringing pain relief and life-saving treatment to the scene, often within the first hour. A small team of well-trained and dedicated enthusiasts will use specially designed stretchers, patient-monitoring machines and sometimes even a helicopter to treat and safely transport the casualty down to a waiting ambulance or even directly to hospital.

The transition has been slow but steadily driven by the ever-increasing number of visitors to the area and the higher and higher expectations of the public. Nearly every aspect of rescue has changed in the last sixty years through technical developments in communications, materials and methods of working and the PDMRO has been at the heart of this development. However, one single thread running through the whole metamorphosis is that of the selfless dedication of the volunteer. It is the enthusiasm and determination of countless ordinary people that have created a service that everyone can be proud of.

It started with an ethos of self-help and that theme continues today with rescue team members being first and foremost lovers of the hills. These people will often have been to the same remote places and climbed the same climbs as the casualties they have turned out to help and after every call-out they will reflect and perhaps think 'That could have been me'.

There have been many landmarks in the development of the service and many people stand out as having done that special bit more. Some have been officially recognised for their individual efforts, either on the hill or in frontline support of the organisation; others have worked just as hard but in the background and out of the limelight. In 2002 all team members with over five years' service received the Queen's Golden Jubilee Medal for their commitment to a frontline emergency service. However, the key word in mountain rescue is 'team' and it has been the team effort since 1933 that has built the Peak District Mountain Rescue Organisation that is so respected today.

Being surrounded by cities such as Manchester, Sheffield, Derby and Stoke, and with many other towns such as Huddersfield, Stockport and Oldham all within a short drive, it is little surprise to find that the Peak District National Park is one of the most visited national parks in the world. In 2000 The Countryside and Rights of Way Act passed through Parliament and came into practical force in September 2004, giving ramblers general access (subject to certain restrictions) to most areas of uncultivated land. The future right to be able to appreciate the beauties of the Peak District National Park and to exercise, play or just simply ramble there is assured.

Just as assured is the fact that visitors to the park will continue to have accidents and so the rescue teams will always be needed. There are now regularly over 200 recorded incidents in the Peak District each year. Technology will continue to move on and the future may bring all sorts of gadgets to help find, treat and even carry a casualty off the hill but, when the weather is foul and the sky is dark, the chances are that the members of one of the PDMRO teams will still have to pull on their boots to answer the rescue call.

Life is mostly froth and bubble,
Two things stand like stone,
Kindness in another's trouble,
Courage in your own.

Ye Wearie Wayfarer, Adam Lindsey Gordon (1833–70)

If mountain rescue in the UK is to remain in the hands of the volunteers who care about the service and who want to carry on the traditions of helping others for no other reason than the pride of a job well done, they need your help. Just enter 'mountain rescue' into any Internet search engine and the World Wide Web will take you to your nearest team.

Dear Guys,
Thank you all very much for your help in getting us off Kinder Scout on 17th August, it was very much appreciated. You're all heroes, or better still, heroes with Mars Bars!
Thank you.

the Search and resquie team!!! They gave us some Jackets and mars bar yum (Mars bars are my favourites) I got to hold a Searh and requie mans hand he was called Nick. my brothe Ollie had a shoulder ride.

Above left: 'Heroes with Mars Bars!'

Abov right: A special letter from a seven year old.

Right: Well dressing is a traditional summer craft in Derbyshire which revives an originally pagan and later Christian ceremony giving thanks for the purity of the spring water. Many thousands of flower petals are pressed onto a clay base to create stunning scenes which, sadly, are only displayed for a few days. 2004 marked the fortieth anniversary of the Peak District Mountain Rescue Organisation and a well in Whaley Bridge and another in Buxton were dressed in celebration of the event.

Other titles published by The History Press

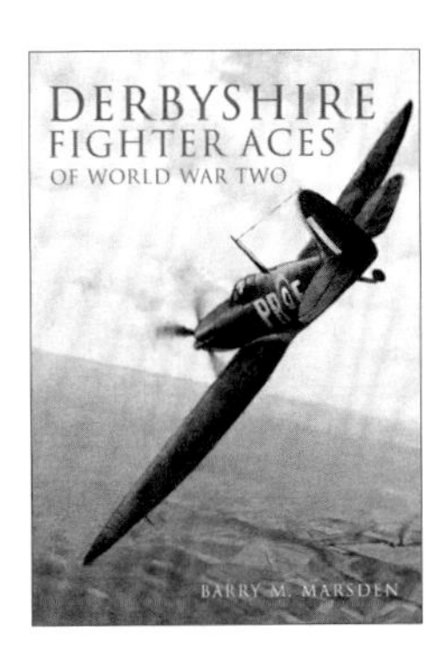

Derbyshire Fighter Aces of World War Two

BARRY M. MARSDEN

From the first day of the Second World War, pilots from Derbyshire were fighting the Germans over France during the Phoney War, and flying in the Battle of Britain and the Western Desert. They fought over Greece, Sicily, Malta and Italy as well as against the Japanese over the Timor Sea. Derbyshiremen flew sweeps, escort duty and fighter-bomber missions into the heart of the Reich. Through bad times and good, they made a world-wide contribution to the inevitable and final defeat of the Axis.

978 0 7524 3173 4

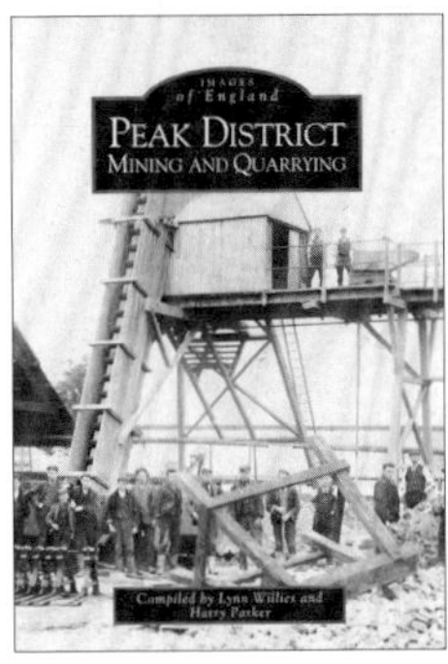

Peak District Mining and Quarrying

LYNN WILLIES AND HARRY PARKER

Open moors, deep valleys, ancient villages and roadways: the Peak District is often looked on as a 'playground' for walkers, climbers and those who come simply to appreciate its beauties. This was also one of England's most important industrial areas, with a history of mining and quarrying stretching back to Roman times and before. However, by the nineteenth century the industry was in decline. Nonetheless, Millclose Mine became Britain's greatest ever lead mine.

978 0 7524 1710 3

Cheshire Life

MIKE EDDISON AND JOHN HOPKINS

These fascinating archive photographs combine views of the county – from urban Macclesfield to the rustic fields of Barrow – with reminders of some of the people who have criss-crossed its landscape and left their mark. All manner of Cheshire life is here. Whatever the image – photograph, print, document, map – all have a story to tell, from the Cheshire farmer 'unlucky in love' to the scribblings of a cheeky schoolboy, or the day that chess Grandmaster Victor Korchnoi met his match in Chester.

978 0 7524 4364 5

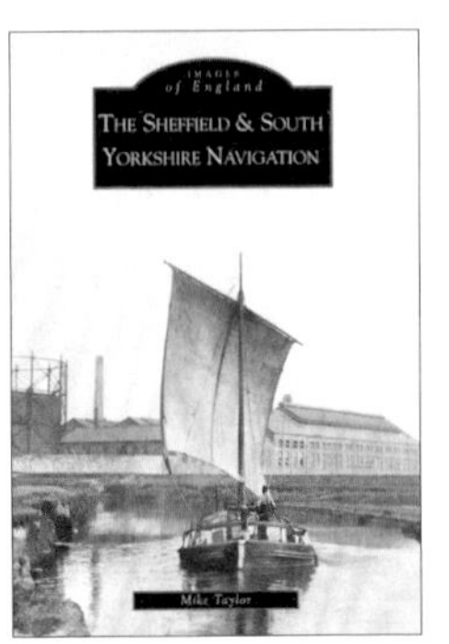

The Sheffield & South Yorkshire Navigation

MIKE TAYLOR

From the improvements around Sheffield at the end of the nineteenth century, through neglect during the First World War, public ownership and the expensive modernisation scheme of the 1980s, as well as the triumphs and failures of private enterprise, The Sheffield & South Yorkshire Navigation documents the history and development of the waterway. Included in this volume is a diverse collection of over 200 images of the navigation, its traffic, and of the surrounding area.

978 0 7524 2128 5

If you are interested in purchasing other books published by The History Press, or in case you have difficulty finding any of our books in your local bookshop, you can also place orders directly through our website

www.thehistorypress.co.uk